Hani Bashier

MSD at a Glance

Market System Development

2023

Publisher:

Säästva OÜ
Hani Bashier
Tartu mnt 67/1-3B
Tallinn
Harju County
10115
https://hani.ee
hani@hani.ee

Library of Congress Control Number: 2023917549

© Hani Bashier

Table of Contents

Abbreviations 2
MSD at a Glance 4
Chapter One 5
Introduction: 5
    Market System Development Approach 5
  Key Principles of the Market System Development Approach 5
    Systems Thinking 5
    Market Facilitation 6
    Inclusivity 6
    Sustainability 6
  Benefits of the Market System Development Approach 6
    Scalability 6
    Adaptability 6
    Efficiency 7
    Sustainability 7
  Application of the Market System Development Approach 7
  Understanding Market System Development (MSD) 7
  Historical Context and Evolution of MSD 9
    Early Development Approaches 9
    Emergence of Market-Led Approaches 10
    Critiques and the Rise of MSD 10
    Systems Thinking and MSD 10
    Evolution of MSD Principles 10
    Integration of Technology and Innovation 11

    Learning and Adaptation 11

Market Systems and Their Components 12

    Market Players 12

    Market Infrastructure 12

    Market Rules and Regulations 13

    Market Information 13

    Market Support Functions 13

    Market Linkages 13

Market Failure and Constraints 14

    Externalities 14

    Monopoly Power 15

    Information Asymmetry 15

    Public Goods 15

    Income Inequality 15

Enabling Environment for Market Development 16

    Stable Legal and Regulatory Framework 16

Access to Finance 17

Infrastructure Development: Infrastructure, including transportation, energy, and communication networks, plays a vital role in market development. Adequate and reliable infrastructure reduces transaction costs, improves connectivity, and enhances productivity. An enabling environment prioritizes infrastructure development and encourages public-private partnerships to ensure efficient and sustainable infrastructure provision. 17

    Skilled Workforce and Human Capital Development 17

    Good Governance and Anti-Corruption Measures 18

- Market Information and Access to Markets 18
- The Role of Market Facilitation in MSD 19
  - Enabling Environment 19
  - Collaboration and Coordination 19
  - Capacity Building 20
  - Market Analysis and Research 20
  - Systemic Change 20
- Market Facilitation Approaches and Techniques 21
  - Participatory Market Systems Development 21
  - Value Chain Development 21
  - Business Development Services 22
  - Innovation and Adaptation 22
  - Monitoring and Learning 22
- Identifying and Analyzing Market Constraints 23
  - Conducting Market Assessments 23
  - Engaging with Market Actors 24
  - Analyzing Market Systems 24
  - Applying Root Cause Analysis 24
  - Prioritizing Constraints 24

Chapter Two 26
Market Assessment and Analysis in MSD 26
- Understanding Market Systems 26
- Identifying Constraints and Opportunities 26
- Stakeholder Engagement 27
- Tools and Approaches 27

- Data-Driven Decision Making 27
- Conducting a Market Assessment 28
  - Define the Objective 28
  - Identify Target Market Segments 28
  - Gather Data 28
  - Analyze Competitors 29
  - Assess Customer Needs 29
  - Evaluate Market Potential 29
  - Make Data-Driven Decisions 29
- Purpose and Objectives of Market Assessment 30
  - Identify Market Potential 30
  - Understand Customer Needs 30
  - Analyze Competitor Landscape 31
  - Assess Market Risks and Challenges 31
  - Support Strategic Decision-making 31
- Data Collection and Analysis Techniques 32
- Data Collection Techniques: 32
  - Surveys 32
  - Interviews 32
  - Observations 33
  - Focus Groups 33
- Data Analysis Techniques 33
  - Descriptive Analysis 33
  - Inferential Analysis 33
  - Qualitative Analysis 33

    Data Visualization 34

    Statistical Analysis 34

    Identifying Market Opportunities and Challenges.............34

    Understanding the Market System 34

    Recognizing Market Opportunities 35

    Assessing Market Challenges 35

    Engaging Stakeholders 35

    Promoting Systemic Change...35

Market Mapping and Stakeholder Analysis 36

    Market Mapping..36

    Stakeholder Analysis 37

    Identifying Key Players 37

    Assessing Interests and Influences.....................................38

    Enhancing Decision-Making 38

Mapping Market Actors and Relationships............................39

    Identifying Key Market Actors..39

    Analyzing Relationships..40

    Understanding Power Dynamics 40

    Identifying Opportunities and Risks 40

    Enhancing Decision-Making 41

Analyzing Stakeholder Interests and Influence......................41

    Identifying Stakeholders...42

    Understanding Interests...42

    Assessing Influence 42

    Managing Relationships 43

Mitigating Risks 43
　　　Enhancing Decision-Making 43
　Engaging Key Stakeholders in MSD Interventions 44
　　　Identifying Key Stakeholders 44
　　　Building Relationships and Trust 44
　　　Involving Stakeholders in Decision-Making 45
　　　Collaborative Problem-Solving 45
　　　Providing Education and Training 45
　　　Continuous Feedback and Evaluation 45
　Understanding Market Systems Dynamics 46
　　　Identifying Key Players and Relationships 47
　　　Analyzing Supply and Demand Dynamics 47
　　　Monitoring Market Trends and Forces 47
　　　Building Strategic Partnerships 47
　　　Anticipating and Managing Risks 48
　Feedback Loops and Interdependencies in Markets 49
　Adapting to Change and Uncertainty in Market Systems 51
　Assessing Market System Resilience and Sustainability 53
　　　Diversity and Redundancy 54
　　　Adaptive Capacity 54
　　　Social Cohesion 54
　　　Environmental Stewardship 54
　　　Governance and Institutions 54
Chapter Three 56
Market Transformation 56

- Strategies for Market Transformation 56
  - Education and Awareness 56
  - Regulatory and Policy Interventions 56
  - Collaboration and Partnerships..57
  - Market-Based Instruments..57
  - Innovation and Technology 57
  - Consumer Demand and Behavior Change 57
- Promoting inclusive growth in Market Systems 58
  - Increasing Access to Markets 58
  - Supporting Small and Medium Enterprises (SMEs) 59
  - Enhancing Skills and Education 59
  - Addressing Social and Gender Inequalities 59
  - Promoting Collaboration and Partnerships.......................59
- Addressing Gender and Social Inequalities 60
  - Education and Awareness 60
  - Policy and Legal Reforms..61
  - Empowering Marginalized Communities 61
  - Promoting Gender Equality in the Workplace 61
  - Collaboration and Partnerships..62
  - Reaching Marginalized and Vulnerable Groups.................62
  - Identifying Barriers 63
  - Tailored Approaches..63
  - Building Trust and Relationships 63
  - Accessible Services and Infrastructure................................63
  - Empowering and Building Capacities 64

8

- Enhancing Access to Opportunities for All 64
  - Identifying Barriers 65
  - Inclusive Policies and Legislation 65
  - Education and Skills Development 65
  - Empowering Marginalized Communities 65
  - Collaboration and Partnerships 66
- Sustainable Business Development and Environmental Considerations 66
  - Environmental Impact Assessment 67
  - Resource Efficiency 67
  - Supply Chain Management 67
  - Stakeholder Engagement 67
  - Corporate Social Responsibility 68
- Integrating Environmental Sustainability in Market Systems 68
  - Sustainable Production Practices 69
  - Sustainable Supply Chains 69
  - Eco-friendly Products and Services 69
  - Green Marketing Strategies 70
  - Long-term Benefits 70
- Promoting Climate Resilience and Green Technologies 71
  - Climate Resilience 71
  - Green Technologies 72
  - Benefits of Promoting Climate Resilience and Green Technologies 72
  - International Cooperation 73

Balancing Economic Growth with Environmental Conservation 73
    Sustainable Development 74
    Environmental Conservation 74
    Economic Growth 74
    Importance of Balance 75
    Strategies for Balancing Economic Growth and Environmental Conservation 75

Leveraging Technology and Innovation in MSD 76
    Enhancing Efficiency 76
    Scaling Impact 77
    Promoting Inclusivity 77
    Fostering Collaboration 77
    Addressing Emerging Challenges 77

Digital Transformation and Market Systems 78
    Enhancing Efficiency 79
    Enabling Inclusive Market Systems 79
    Facilitating Data-Driven Decision-Making 79
    Fostering Innovation and Collaboration 80
    Building Resilient Market Systems 80

Harnessing Mobile Technology and E-commerce 81
Importance of Mobile Technology in MSD 81
Leveraging E-commerce in MSD 81
Benefits of Harnessing Mobile Technology and E-commerce in MSD 82
    Enhanced Convenience 82

- Improved Efficiency ... 82
- Personalized Experiences ... 82
- Increased Reach ... 82
- Data-driven Decision Making ... 82
- Competitive Advantage ... 83
- Fostering Innovation and Entrepreneurship in Markets ... 83
- Importance of Fostering Innovation and Entrepreneurship ... 83
  - Economic Growth ... 84
  - Competitiveness ... 84
  - Problem Solving ... 84
  - Job Creation ... 84
  - Resilience ... 84
- Chapter Four ... 86
- Policy and Advocacy for Market Systems Development ... 86
  - Importance of Policy and Advocacy in MSD ... 86
    - Enabling Environment ... 86
    - Systemic Change ... 86
    - Collaboration and Coordination ... 87
    - Scaling Up and Replication ... 87
  - Understanding Policy and Regulatory Frameworks ... 88
  - Components of Policy and Regulatory Frameworks in MSD ... 88
    - Legal and Regulatory Frameworks ... 88
    - Sector-Specific Policies ... 88
    - Institutional Arrangements ... 88
    - Monitoring and Evaluation Mechanisms ... 89

Policy and Regulatory Challenges in MSD 89
    Lack of Capacity 89
    Coordination and Collaboration 89
    Balancing Interests 89
    Policy Inertia 90
Role of Government in Market Systems 90
    Creating an Enabling Environment 90
    Promoting Inclusive Growth 91
    Regulation and Oversight 91
    Facilitating Collaboration and Coordination 92
Policy Formulation and Implementation Processes 92
    Policy Formulation 93
    Policy Implementation 93

Importance of Policy Formulation and Implementation in MSD: 94

Effective policy formulation and implementation are critical for the success of MSD. Well-designed policies can create an enabling environment that supports market systems development, attracts investments, and stimulates economic growth. Policies that promote inclusive growth help reduce poverty, create employment opportunities, and improve the livelihoods of individuals and communities. They can also contribute to sustainable development by addressing environmental challenges and promoting responsible business practices. 94

    Creating Enabling Policy Environment for Market Development: 95
    Understanding an Enabling Policy Environment: 95

The Role of Policy in Market Development 96

Key Considerations in Policy Formulation 96

Implementation and Monitoring 96

Benefits of an Enabling Policy Environment 97

Building Alliances and Coalitions for Advocacy 98

The Power of Alliances and Coalitions: Building alliances and coalitions is essential for effective advocacy in MSD. By joining forces with like-minded organizations, stakeholders, and networks, MSD practitioners can amplify their voices, share resources, and leverage collective expertise to advocate for policy reforms and inclusive market practices. These partnerships have the potential to create a stronger and more unified advocacy front, increasing the likelihood of success in driving systemic change. 98

Strategies for Building Alliances and Coalitions 98

Identify Shared Goals and Objectives 99

Engage in Collaborative Planning 99

Establish Trust and Communication 99

Leverage Diverse Expertise 99

Advocate for Mutual Interests 100

Engage in Joint Advocacy Activities 100

Engaging with Policy Makers and Influencers 100

The Importance of Engaging with Policy Makers and Influencers 101

Strategies for Effective Engagement 101

Build Relationships 101

Demonstrate the Value of MSD 101

Tailor Messages to the Audience 102

- Collaborate in Policy Development 102
- Leverage Influencers and Networks 102
- Continuously Monitor and Evaluate 102
- Communicating the Benefits of MSD to Stakeholders 103
- Importance of Communicating MSD Benefits 104
  - Alignment of Expectations 104
  - Support and Buy-In 104
  - Overcoming Resistance to Change 104
- Monitoring and Evaluation of MSD Programs 105
- Importance of Monitoring and Evaluation 105
  - Tracking Progress 105
  - Accountability and Learning 106
- Key Aspects of Effective M&E in MSD Programs 106
  - Clear Objectives and Indicators 106
  - Data Collection and Analysis 106
  - Continuous Feedback and Adaptation 107
- Developing Monitoring and Evaluation Frameworks 107
- Importance of Developing M&E Frameworks 108
  - Clear Objectives and Target 108
  - Accountability and Learning 108
  - Evidence-Based Decision-Making 108
- Key Considerations for Developing M&E Frameworks in MSD 108
  - Data Collection and Analysis 109
  - Regular Monitoring and Evaluation 109

- Indicators and Measurement of Market System Change 110
- Importance of Indicators and Measurement 110
  - Tracking Change in Market Systems 110
  - Assessing Impact and Effectiveness 111
  - Accountability and Learning 111
- Key Considerations for Indicators and Measurement in MSD 111
  - Relevance and Alignment 111
  - Data Collection and Analysis 112
  - Participatory Approach 112
- Learning and Adaptation in MSD Interventions 113
- Importance of Learning and Adaptation 113
  - Flexibility and Responsiveness 113
  - Maximizing Impact 113
  - Collaboration and Knowledge Sharing 114
- Key Considerations for Learning and Adaptation in MSD Interventions 114
  - Monitoring and Evaluation 114
  - Participatory Approach 114
  - Knowledge Management and Learning Platforms 115

Chapter Five 116

Case Studies in Market System Development 116
- Successful MSD Interventions in Agriculture Sector 116
- Impact of MSD Interventions in Agriculture 116
  - Increased Productivity and Income 116
  - Strengthened Market Linkages 117

Improved Resilience and Adaptability 117
Improving Agricultural Value Chain 117
Potential Benefits of Improved Agricultural Value Chains...118
    Increased Incomes for Farmers...118
    Enhanced Food Security and Nutrition 118
    Sustainable Agricultural Practices.....................................118
    Enhancing Access to Inputs and Finance..........................119
Strengthening Farmer Organizations and Cooperatives......120
Importance of Strengthening Farmer Organizations and Cooperatives..120
    Enhancing Farmer Voice and Representation..................120
    Building Market Power and Negotiating Strength...........121
    Facilitating Knowledge Sharing and Capacity Building 121
Key Strategies in Strengthening Farmer Organizations and Cooperatives..121
    Institutional Strengthening and Governance...................121
    Market Linkages and Access to Services 122
    Advocacy and Networking..122
MSD Approaches in Micro, Small, and Medium Enterprises (MSMEs) 122
Promoting MSMEs in Urban and Rural Areas 123
    Urban Areas..123
Market System Development in Conflict-Affected Areas 126
Addressing Market Disruptions and Fragilities 127
Building Resilience and Economic Recovery 128
Promoting Peacebuilding through Market Development....128

Economic Opportunities...129
Trade and Interdependence...129
Reintegration and Reconciliation 130
Infrastructure Development 130
Social and Economic Inclusion 130

Chapter Six..132

Partnerships and Collaboration.................................132

Engaging with Private Sector in MSD Initiatives 132
Engaging with Private Sector in MSD Initiatives 133
Corporate Social Responsibility and Shared Value Approaches
....134
Corporate Social Responsibility (CSR) 134
Shared Value...134
Benefits of CSR and Shared Value approaches 135
Enhanced Reputation 135
Increased Employee Engagement......................................135
Improved Risk Management 135
Access to New Markets 135
Long-term Sustainability 135
Public-Private Partnerships for Market Development.........136
Cross-Sector Collaboration in MSD 137
Enhanced Knowledge and Expertise 137
Holistic and Integrated Approaches...................................138
Coordinated and Aligned Efforts..138
Increased Accountability and Ownership 138

17

- Leveraging Resources and Networks 139
- Policy Coherence and Systemic Change 139
- Collaboration between Government and Civil Society Organizations 140
- Importance of Collaboration between Government and CSOs: 140
  - Citizen Participation 140
  - Policy Development and Implementation 141
  - Service Delivery and Accountability 141
  - Advocacy and Social Justice 141
  - Harmonizing Efforts of Development Practitioners 142
- The benefits of harmonizing efforts extend to both development practitioners and the communities they serve 142
- International Cooperation and Funding Mechanisms for MSD 143
  - Official Development Assistance (ODA) 144
  - Multilateral Development Banks (MDBs) 144
  - Public-Private Partnerships (PPPs) 144
  - Impact Investing 144
- Bilateral and Multilateral Aid Agencies in Market Development 145
- Innovative Financing Models for MSD Programs 148
- Coordinating Donor Support for Market System Transformation 148

Chapter Seven 151
Scaling up and Replicating Successful MSD Interventions 151

The Importance of Scaling up and Replicating MSD
Interventions 151
Strategies for Effective Scaling up and Replication 151
    Document and Share Best Practices 152
    Strengthen Partnerships and Collaboration 152
    Adapt Interventions to Local Contexts 152
    Build Local Capacity 152
    Monitor, Evaluate, and Learn 153
    Advocate for Policy Change 153
    Identifying Scalable Interventions in Market Systems 154
    Importance of Identifying Scalable Interventions 154
Strategies for Identifying Scalable Interventions 154
    Market Analysis 154
    Evidence and Data-driven Approach 155
    Stakeholder Engagement 155
    Systemic Approach 155
    Innovation and Adaptation 156
    Risk Assessment 156
Replication of Successful MSD Models 157
Importance of Replication 157
    Scalability 157
    Efficiency 157
    Learning and Adaptation 157
    Evidence-based Approach 158
Challenges in Replication 158

Contextual Adaptation 158
Capacity Building 158
Sustainability 158
Documenting and Sharing Best Practices in MSD 159
Importance of Documentation and Sharing......................... 159
Learning and Improvement... 160
Replication and Scaling.. 160
Evidence-based Decision Making 160
Building a Community of Practice 160
Challenges in Documenting and Sharing.............................. 160
Capturing Tacit Knowledge 160
Time and Resource Constraints....................................... 161
Ensuring Relevance and Applicability.............................. 161
Factors to Consider in Adaptation.. 162
1) .... Contextual Analysis
.... 162
2) .... Stakeholder Engagement
.... 162
3) .... Flexibility and Iteration
.... 162
4) .... Risk Management
.... 163
Promoting South-South Collaboration in Market System
Development 163
Benefits of South-South Collaboration 164
Shared Context and Similar Challenges........................... 164

- Knowledge Exchange and Learning 164
- Capacity Building and Skill Transfer 164
- Networking and Regional Integration 165
- Key Elements for Successful Collaboration 165
  - Shared Vision and Objectives 165
  - Mutual Trust and Respect 165
  - Effective Communication and Coordination 165
  - Resource Sharing and Mutual Support 165
- Examples of Successful South-South Collaboration Initiatives 166
  - Africa Exchange Network (AFEX) 166
  - ASEAN Integration Initiative for ASEAN Economic Community (AEC) 166
  - Latin American and Caribbean Network for Small and Medium Enterprise Development (RED-PYME) 166
- Monitoring and Sustaining Market System Transformation 167
- Why Monitor Market System Transformation? 168
- Strategies for Monitoring and Sustaining Market System Transformation 168
  - Establish Baseline Data 168
  - Stakeholder Engagement 169
  - Continuous Learning and Adaptation 169
  - Capacity Building 169
  - Collaboration and Partnerships 169
- Long-term Monitoring and Evaluation of MSD Programs 170

- Why is Long-term Monitoring and Evaluation Important? 171
- Ensuring Continuity and Sustainability of Market Changes .172
- Why is Continuity and Sustainability Important? 172
- Transferring Ownership to Local Institutions and Stakeholders 173

Chapter Eight 174
Future Directions and Emerging Trends in MSD 174
- Embracing Digital Transformation 174
- Addressing Climate Change and Sustainability 174
- Promoting Gender Equality and Social Inclusion 175
- Strengthening Collaboration and Partnerships................175
- Leveraging Data and Analytics 176
- Innovations in Technology and Digital Transformation 176
  - E-commerce Platforms 177
  - Mobile Applications and Payment Systems 177
  - Internet of Things (IoT)...177
  - Artificial Intelligence (AI) and Machine Learning (ML).....178
  - Blockchain Technology 178
  - Data Analytics and Visualization 178
  - Cloud Computing..178
  - Social media and Digital Marketing..................................179
- Blockchain and Distributed Ledger Technology in Market Systems...179
  - Enhanced Transparency and Trust...................................180
  - Improved Security and Data Integrity 180

- Streamlined Supply Chain Management 180
- Efficient Financial Transactions 181
- Decentralized Marketplaces 181
- Intellectual Property Rights Protection 181
- Tokenization and Crowdfunding 182

Artificial Intelligence and Data Analytics for Market Development 182
- Data-Driven Decision Making 183
- Market Intelligence and Research 183
- Targeted Interventions 183
- Predictive Analytics 184
- Automation and Efficiency 184
- Risk Assessment and Mitigation 184
- Continuous Monitoring and Evaluation 185

Fine-tech and Digital Financial Inclusion in MSD 185
- Digital Payments and Mobile Money 186
- Access to Credit and Financing 186
- Financial Literacy and Education 186
- Insurance and Risk Management 187
- Digital Identity and KYC 187
- Partnerships and Collaboration 187
- Data Analytics and Market Insights 188

Climate Change and Resilience in Market Systems 188
Understanding Climate Risks 189
- Diversification and Adaptation 189

  Access to Climate Finance 189

  Strengthening Value Chains 190

  Knowledge Sharing and Capacity Building 190

  Stakeholder Collaboration................................. 190

  Policy and Regulatory Support 191

Adapting Market Systems to Climate Change Impacts 191

  Understanding the Need for Adaptation 192

  Building Resilient Supply Chains......................... 192

  Promoting Sustainable Agriculture and Production 193

  Encouraging Green Innovation and Technology 193

  Enhancing Financial Mechanisms..................... 193

Promoting Climate-Smart Agriculture and Renewable Energy Markets.. 194

  Climate-Smart Agriculture................................. 195

  Renewable Energy Markets................................. 195

  Synergies between Climate-Smart Agriculture and Renewable Energy 196

Building Resilience in Vulnerable Communities through MSD 197

Benefits of Building Resilience through MSD........................ 198

  Poverty reduction 198

  Inclusive growth 198

  Empowerment... 198

  Risk reduction 198

  Sustainable development................................. 199

Challenges and Considerations 199

    Complex systems 199

    Stakeholder coordination 199

    Long-term commitment 199

    Risk of unintended consequences 199

Addressing Inequality and Social Inclusion in MSD 200

Understanding Inequality in the Context of MSD 200

Promoting Social Inclusion in MSD 201

    Inclusive market assessments 201

    Stakeholder engagement 201

    Capacity building 201

    Access to finance and resources 201

    Gender mainstreaming 202

Monitoring and Evaluation for Social Inclusion 202

Collaboration and Partnerships 202

Gender Mainstreaming and Women's Economic Empowerment 203

Gender Mainstreaming in MSD 203

Importance of Women's Economic Empowerment 204

Strategies for Gender Mainstreaming and Women's Economic Empowerment in MSD 204

    Gender-responsive market assessments 204

    Capacity building for women 204

    Access to finance and assets 204

    Gender-inclusive value chain development 205

    Promoting women's leadership and decision-making 205

    Engaging men and changing social norms 205

Monitoring and Evaluation for Gender Mainstreaming 205
Inclusive Business Models in MSD 206
   Importance of Disability-Inclusive Market Systems 207
   Strategies for Inclusive Business Models and Disability-Inclusive Market Systems in MSD: 207
   Accessibility and Universal Design 207
   Disability-Inclusive Value Chains 207
   Skills Development and Capacity Building 208
Monitoring and Evaluation for Inclusive Business Models .. 208
Promoting Youth Entrepreneurship and Employment in Markets 209
   Importance of Youth Entrepreneurship and Employment in Markets 209
   Strategies for Promoting Youth Entrepreneurship and Employment in Markets 210
   Entrepreneurship Education and Training 210
   Access to Finance and Business Support Services 210
   Creating a Supportive Entrepreneurial Ecosystem 210
   Skills Development and Vocational Training 211
   Networking and Collaboration Opportunities 211
Monitoring and Evaluation for Youth Entrepreneurship and Employment 211
Chapter Nine 213
Application Areas of Market System Development Approach 213
   Agriculture and Rural Development 213
   Financial Inclusion and Access to Finance 213

    Employment and Skills Development 214

    Trade and Market Access 214

    Micro, Small, and Medium Enterprises (MSMEs) Development 214

    Women's Economic Empowerment 215

Application of MSD for IDPs 216

    Livelihoods and Income Generation 216

    Access to Basic Services 216

    Shelter and Housing 217

    Market Integration and Social Cohesion 217

    Access to Justice and Legal Services 218

Application of MSD for Refugees 218

    Livelihoods and Income Generation 219

    Access to Basic Services 219

    Housing and Shelter 220

    Market Integration and Social Cohesion 220

    Access to Education and Skills Development 221

Application of MSD for Returnees and Host Communities .. 221

    Livelihoods and Economic Recovery 222

    Infrastructure Development 222

    Access to Basic Services 223

    Market Integration and Social Cohesion 223

    Entrepreneurship and Skills Development 224

Abbreviations

AEC	ASEAN Integration Initiative for ASEAN Economic Community
AFEX	Africa Exchange Network
AI	Artificial Intelligence
BLT	Blockchain and Distributed Ledger Technology
CSO	Civil Society Organization
CSR	Corporate Social Responsibility
CSR	Corporate Social Responsibility
DFID	Department for International Development (UK)
ICT	Information and Communication Technology
IDP	Internally Displaced Person
IMF	International Monetary Fund
IoT	Internet of Things
KYC	Know Your Customer
M&E	Monitoring & Evaluation
MDB	Multilateral Development Banks
ML	Machine Learning
MSD	Market System Development
MSP	Multi-stakeholder platform
NGO	Non-Governmental Organization
ODA	Official Development Assistance
PPP	Public-Private Partnerships
RED-PYME	Latin American and Caribbean Network for Small and Medium Enterprise Development
SIB	Social Impact Bond
SMART	Specific, Measurable, Achievable, Relevant, and Time-bound
SMEs	Small and Medium-sized Enterprises
UNDP	United Nations Development Program
USAID	United States Agency for International Development

MSD at a Glance

The Market System Development (MSD) approach is a comprehensive framework used to promote economic growth and poverty reduction in developing countries. It recognizes that vibrant and inclusive markets are essential for sustainable development. The MSD approach aims to strengthen market systems by addressing market failures and improving the enabling environment.

Key principles of the MSD approach include market facilitation, collaboration, and systemic change. Market facilitation involves working with market actors to identify and address constraints that hinder market functioning. Collaboration is emphasized by bringing together a diverse range of stakeholders, including private sector actors, government agencies, civil society organizations, and development practitioners. Systemic change focuses on addressing underlying structural issues within market systems to promote long-term transformation and sustainability.

The MSD approach employs a range of tools and interventions, such as market assessments, capacity building, policy advocacy, and financial services. It promotes inclusive growth by targeting marginalized groups, promoting gender equality, and ensuring environmental sustainability. By adopting the MSD approach, policymakers and practitioners can foster resilient and dynamic market systems that create opportunities, enhance competitiveness, and improve livelihoods for individuals and communities in developing countries.

Chapter One

Introduction:

Market System Development Approach

Market System Development (MSD) approach is a framework used to address developmental challenges and promote economic growth in low-income countries. It focuses on improving market systems by addressing market failures and constraints that hinder economic development. In this article, we will explore the key concepts and principles of the MSD approach, its benefits, and its application in achieving sustainable development.

Understanding the Market System Development Approach

The MSD approach recognizes that markets are complex systems influenced by various stakeholders, institutions, and external factors. It aims to create an enabling environment that allows market actors to interact, innovate, and thrive. Rather than implementing traditional aid or intervention programs, the MSD approach emphasizes market-based solutions and interventions that strengthen the underlying market system.

Key Principles of the Market System Development Approach

Systems Thinking: The MSD approach takes a holistic view of the market system, considering the interactions, dynamics, and feedback loops between different actors and components. It recognizes that changes in one part of the system can have ripple effects throughout.

Market Facilitation: Instead of directly providing goods or services, the MSD approach focuses on facilitating market transactions and creating an environment that encourages private sector investment, competition, and innovation.

Inclusivity: The MSD approach aims to ensure that marginalized groups, such as women, youth, and the poor, have equal access to market opportunities and benefits.

Sustainability: The MSD approach prioritizes long-term impact and sustainability by strengthening local institutions, building local capacity, and promoting ownership and responsibility among local stakeholders.

Benefits of the Market System Development Approach

The MSD approach offers several benefits in promoting sustainable economic development:

Scalability: By targeting systemic constraints, the MSD approach has the potential to create broader, long-lasting impacts that extend beyond individual projects or interventions.

Adaptability: The MSD approach is flexible and adaptable to different contexts and sectors. It recognizes that each market system is unique and requires tailored interventions.

Efficiency: By leveraging existing market mechanisms and resources, the MSD approach maximizes efficiency and cost-effectiveness.

Sustainability: The focus on building local capacity and ownership ensures that interventions are sustainable even after external support is phased out.

Application of the Market System Development Approach

The MSD approach has been successfully applied in various sectors, including agriculture, finance, healthcare, and energy. For example, in the agriculture sector, the MSD approach may involve strengthening input supply chains, improving access to finance for smallholder farmers, and promoting market linkages between farmers and buyers. In the healthcare sector, the MSD approach may focus on improving the efficiency and affordability of healthcare services by addressing market failures in the supply chain or incentivizing private sector investment in underserved areas.

The Market System Development approach offers a comprehensive and sustainable framework for addressing developmental challenges and promoting economic growth. By focusing on strengthening market systems and facilitating market-based solutions, the MSD approach enables long-term impact and empowers local stakeholders to drive their own development.

Understanding Market System Development (MSD)

Market System Development (MSD) is an approach that aims to promote sustainable economic growth and alleviate poverty by strengthening market systems in low-income countries. It recognizes that markets are complex, interconnected systems influenced by various factors and stakeholders. By addressing market failures and constraints, the MSD approach seeks to create an enabling environment that allows market actors to thrive and generate positive impacts.

At its core, the MSD approach adopts a holistic view of market systems, considering the interactions and dynamics between different actors, institutions, and external factors. It emphasizes the importance of systems thinking, recognizing that changes in one part of the system can have ripple effects throughout. This approach moves away from traditional aid or intervention programs and focuses on market-based solutions and interventions that strengthen the underlying market system.

Key principles guide the implementation of the MSD approach. These principles include market facilitation, inclusivity, sustainability, and adaptability. Market facilitation involves creating an environment that encourages private sector investment, competition, and innovation. Inclusivity ensures that marginalized groups have equal access to market opportunities. Sustainability is achieved by building local capacity, strengthening institutions, and promoting ownership among local stakeholders. Adaptability allows for tailoring interventions to specific contexts and sectors, recognizing the uniqueness of each market system.

The benefits of the MSD approach are numerous. It offers scalability, allowing for broader and long-lasting impacts that extend beyond individual projects. By leveraging existing market mechanisms and resources, the MSD approach maximizes efficiency and cost-effectiveness. Furthermore, sustainability is emphasized through the focus on building local capacity and ownership, ensuring that interventions can be maintained even after external support is phased out.

Overall, understanding the Market System Development approach is crucial for addressing developmental challenges and fostering sustainable economic growth. By strengthening market systems and facilitating market-based solutions, the MSD approach empowers local stakeholders to drive their own development and create lasting positive change.

Historical Context and Evolution of MSD

Market System Development (MSD) has evolved over time as a response to the changing understanding of development and poverty alleviation. The approach has its roots in the broader field of economic development, which has undergone significant shifts in theory and practice throughout history.

Early Development Approaches: In the mid-20th century, development efforts focused primarily on infrastructure and large-scale projects led by governments. The dominant belief was that economic growth would automatically lead to poverty reduction. However, it became evident that these top-down approaches did not always benefit the most marginalized populations.

Emergence of Market-Led Approaches: In the 1980s and 1990s, there was a shift towards market-led approaches to development. This shift was influenced by the rise of neoliberal economic policies and the belief that markets, if left to function freely, would generate growth and alleviate poverty. This approach initially focused on macroeconomic reforms and liberalization.

Critiques and the Rise of MSD: Over time, it became clear that simply relying on market forces was insufficient to address poverty and inequality. Critics argued that market-led approaches neglected the structural barriers and market failures that perpetuated poverty. In response to these critiques, the MSD approach emerged as a way to address these issues.

Systems Thinking and MSD: MSD is rooted in the concept of systems thinking, which gained prominence in the late 20th century. It recognizes that markets are complex systems influenced by various actors, institutions, and external factors. MSD acknowledges that interventions need to consider the broader system dynamics and interactions to achieve sustainable change.

Evolution of MSD Principles: The core principles of MSD, including market facilitation, inclusivity, sustainability, and adaptability, have evolved over time. These principles have been refined through practice, research, and learning from successes and failures. The focus has shifted towards building local capacity, strengthening institutions, and promoting ownership among local stakeholders.

Integration of Technology and Innovation: As technology has advanced, MSD has embraced innovation and the use of digital tools to drive economic growth and inclusion. The integration of technology has expanded access to markets, enhanced productivity, and created new opportunities for small-scale entrepreneurs.

Learning and Adaptation: MSD continues to evolve through learning and adaptation. Practitioners and researchers continuously refine their understanding of market systems and develop new approaches to address emerging challenges. Learning networks and knowledge sharing platforms facilitate the exchange of best practices and lessons learned.

The historical context of MSD reflects a shift from top-down development approaches to a more nuanced understanding of market systems and their complexities. The evolution of MSD has been driven by a recognition of the limitations of market-led approaches and a focus on addressing market failures and structural barriers. The approach continues to evolve and adapt as new challenges and opportunities arise, with a growing emphasis on inclusivity, sustainability, and the integration of technology and innovation.

Adopting MSD is vital for achieving sustainable and inclusive economic development. By addressing market failures and promoting systemic change, MSD enables inclusive growth, empowers local communities, builds resilience, and contributes to sustainable development. The benefits extend beyond economic outcomes, fostering social cohesion, environmental sustainability, and collaboration among diverse stakeholders. Embracing MSD approaches will pave the way for more equitable and prosperous societies.

Market Systems and Their Components

Market systems are complex networks of buyers, sellers, rules, and institutions that facilitate the exchange of goods, services, and resources. Understanding the components of market systems is crucial for analyzing how markets function and for designing interventions to promote economic development. Here are the key components of market systems:

Market Players: Market players are the individuals, businesses, and organizations that participate in market transactions. This includes producers, consumers, suppliers, distributors, retailers, and service providers. Market players interact with each other through the buying and selling of goods and services, driving the functioning of the market system.

Market Infrastructure: Market infrastructure refers to the physical and organizational structures that support market transactions. This includes transportation networks, communication systems, storage facilities, financial institutions, and legal frameworks. Market infrastructure plays a vital role in facilitating the smooth flow of goods, information, and capital within the market system.

Market Rules and Regulations: Market rules and regulations are the formal and informal guidelines that govern market behavior. They include laws, regulations, industry standards, and social norms that shape how market players interact. These rules establish the framework for fair competition, consumer protection, property rights, contract enforcement, and dispute resolution.

Market Information: Information is a critical component of market systems. Market players require accurate and timely information on prices, product quality, demand, supply, and market trends to make informed decisions. Access to reliable market information enables market efficiency, transparency, and fair competition.

Market Support Functions: Market support functions provide essential services that enable market transactions to take place. These functions include financial services, business development services, marketing and advertising, market research, and skills development. Market support functions help market players overcome barriers and improve their competitiveness.

Market Linkages: Market linkages refer to the connections and relationships among market players in the market system. These linkages can be vertical (between different stages of the value chain) or horizontal (between similar market players). Strong market linkages promote cooperation, knowledge sharing, and innovation, leading to improved market performance.

Understanding the interplay between these components is crucial for effective market system development. Interventions aimed at strengthening market systems should consider how changes in one component can impact other components. By addressing constraints and improving the functioning of market players, infrastructure, rules and regulations, information, support functions, and linkages, market systems can become more inclusive, efficient, and sustainable.

Market Failure and Constraints

Market failure occurs when the allocation of resources in a market is inefficient, leading to suboptimal outcomes. It happens when the functioning of the market system fails to achieve economic efficiency or when the market does not produce the socially desirable quantity of goods and services. There are several types of market failures, each with its own set of constraints:

Externalities: Externalities are costs or benefits that are not reflected in the market price of a good or service. Positive externalities, such as the provision of public goods or environmental conservation, are under-produced, while negative externalities, like pollution or congestion, are overproduced. The lack of property rights and the difficulty in assigning value to external costs or benefits create constraints in addressing externalities.

Monopoly Power: Monopoly power occurs when a single firm dominates the market and has significant control over prices and output. Monopolies can lead to higher prices, reduced consumer choice, and decreased innovation. The constraint is the lack of competition to regulate prices and ensure efficiency.

Information Asymmetry: Information asymmetry exists when one party in a transaction has more information than the other, leading to unequal power and potential exploitation. This can result in adverse selection, where buyers or sellers have incomplete information about the quality of goods or services, or moral hazard, where one party changes their behavior after the transaction is made. The constraint lies in the difficulty of obtaining and verifying accurate information.

Public Goods: Public goods are non-excludable and non-rivalrous, meaning that individuals cannot be excluded from their benefits, and one person's consumption does not diminish the availability to others. Public goods, such as national defense or street lighting, are typically underprovided by the market due to the free-rider problem, where individuals can benefit without contributing. The constraint is the difficulty in ensuring adequate provision and funding of public goods.

Income Inequality: Market systems can result in income disparities, where some individuals or groups have significantly more resources than others. High levels of income inequality can lead to social and economic instability, limiting opportunities for social mobility and hindering overall economic growth. The constraint is addressing the systemic factors that contribute to income inequality, such as unequal access to education, healthcare, and employment opportunities.

Addressing market failures and constraints often requires government intervention and the implementation of appropriate policies. These can include regulations, taxes or subsidies, public provision of goods and services, antitrust measures, and social safety nets. By recognizing and addressing market failures and constraints, societies can strive for more equitable and efficient outcomes, promoting the well-being of individuals and fostering sustainable economic development.

Enabling Environment for Market Development

Creating an enabling environment for market development is essential for fostering economic growth, attracting investment, and promoting entrepreneurship. An enabling environment refers to the set of conditions, policies, and institutions that facilitate the smooth functioning of markets and encourage private sector participation. Here are some key factors that contribute to an enabling environment for market development:

Stable Legal and Regulatory Framework: A stable legal and regulatory framework provides certainty and predictability for businesses. Clear and transparent laws and regulations protect property rights, enforce contracts, and ensure fair competition. This helps to build trust and confidence among market participants, both domestic and foreign.

Access to Finance: Access to finance is critical for businesses to start, expand, and innovate. An enabling environment promotes a well-functioning financial sector that offers a range of financial products and services, including affordable credit, venture capital, and insurance. It also encourages the development of financial infrastructure, such as credit bureaus and payment systems, to facilitate efficient transactions.

Infrastructure Development: Infrastructure, including transportation, energy, and communication networks, plays a vital role in market development. Adequate and reliable infrastructure reduces transaction costs, improves connectivity, and enhances productivity. An enabling environment prioritizes infrastructure development and encourages public-private partnerships to ensure efficient and sustainable infrastructure provision.

Skilled Workforce and Human Capital Development: A skilled workforce is essential for driving innovation, productivity, and competitiveness in markets. An enabling environment promotes education and training programs that equip individuals with the necessary skills for the labor market. It also encourages lifelong learning and supports the development of a diverse and inclusive workforce.

Good Governance and Anti-Corruption Measures: Good governance, transparency, and accountability are crucial for market development. Effective institutions, including strong legal systems and anti-corruption measures, promote fair competition, prevent market distortions, and ensure the rule of law. An enabling environment fosters a culture of integrity and ethical business practices.

Market Information and Access to Markets: Timely and accurate market information is vital for businesses to make informed decisions and identify market opportunities. An enabling environment provides mechanisms for collecting, analyzing, and disseminating market information. It also promotes access to domestic and international markets, including reducing trade barriers and facilitating trade agreements.

Creating an enabling environment for market development requires collaboration between governments, businesses, civil society, and other stakeholders. It involves a comprehensive approach that addresses various aspects of the business environment. By fostering an enabling environment, countries can attract investment, create jobs, and build sustainable and inclusive markets that contribute to long-term economic growth and development.

The Role of Market Facilitation in MSD

Market facilitation plays a crucial role in the success of Market Systems Development (MSD) programs. MSD aims to promote inclusive economic growth by improving market systems and enabling market actors to better meet the needs of the poor and vulnerable. Market facilitation involves creating an enabling environment, fostering collaboration, and providing targeted support to market actors to drive positive change. In this article, we will explore the importance of market facilitation in MSD and its various roles in achieving sustainable development outcomes.

Enabling Environment: Market facilitators work towards creating an enabling environment for market actors to thrive. This includes addressing policy and regulatory barriers, promoting fair competition, and ensuring access to market information. By removing these obstacles, market facilitators can stimulate market dynamics and encourage innovation and investment.

Collaboration and Coordination: Market facilitators play a crucial role in fostering collaboration and coordination among different market actors. They bring together stakeholders, including producers, suppliers, buyers, and service providers, to identify common goals, build trust, and promote collective action. This collaboration leads to the development of mutually beneficial relationships and the creation of value chains that are more inclusive and resilient.

Capacity Building: Market facilitators provide targeted support and capacity building to market actors to enhance their skills, knowledge, and capabilities. This can include training programs, technical assistance, and access to finance and business development services. By strengthening the capacity of market actors, facilitators empower them to adapt to market changes, improve their productivity, and seize new business opportunities.

Market Analysis and Research: Market facilitators conduct rigorous market analysis and research to understand the dynamics, constraints, and opportunities within specific market systems. This information helps identify market failures, bottlenecks, and potential interventions. Market facilitators also monitor and evaluate the impact of their interventions to continuously learn and adapt their strategies.

Systemic Change: The ultimate goal of market facilitation in MSD is to drive systemic change within market systems. By addressing root causes and systemic constraints, facilitators aim to create sustainable and inclusive market systems that benefit all stakeholders. This involves promoting systemic innovations, influencing policy reforms, and fostering long-term resilience and adaptability.

Market facilitation plays a critical role in Market Systems Development by creating an enabling environment, fostering collaboration, building capacity, conducting market analysis, and driving systemic change. By adopting a facilitative approach, MSD programs can unlock the potential of market systems and create sustainable and inclusive economic growth that benefits the poor and vulnerable.

Market Facilitation Approaches and Techniques

Market facilitation involves implementing various approaches and techniques to effectively support market actors and drive positive change within market systems. These approaches and techniques are designed to foster collaboration, build trust, and enable market actors to adapt and thrive in dynamic market environments. In this article, we will explore some common market facilitation approaches and techniques that are widely used in the field.

Participatory Market Systems Development: This approach emphasizes the active involvement of market actors in identifying and addressing market constraints. Facilitators engage with stakeholders through participatory processes, such as focus group discussions, workshops, and stakeholder mapping exercises. This approach ensures that interventions are demand-driven, context-specific, and aligned with the needs and priorities of market actors.

Value Chain Development: Value chain development focuses on strengthening the relationships and linkages between different actors in a specific market system. Facilitators analyze the value chain to identify key bottlenecks and opportunities for improvement. They then work with market actors to develop strategies to enhance productivity, quality, and market access. This approach aims to create more inclusive and value-added value chains that benefit all actors.

Business Development Services: Facilitators provide targeted business development services to market actors, including training, technical assistance, and access to finance. These services help build the capacity and skills of market actors, enabling them to improve their competitiveness and seize new business opportunities. By addressing knowledge and resource gaps, facilitators empower market actors to adapt to changing market conditions.

Innovation and Adaptation: Market facilitators encourage innovation and adaptation within market systems to drive positive change. They promote the adoption of new technologies, business models, and practices that can improve productivity, efficiency, and sustainability. Facilitators also support the development of networks and platforms for knowledge sharing and learning, enabling market actors to collaborate and innovate collectively.

Monitoring and Learning: Effective market facilitation requires continuous monitoring and learning. Facilitators collect and analyze data on market dynamics, outcomes, and impact to assess the effectiveness of their interventions. They use this information to adapt their strategies, improve their approaches, and share lessons learned with stakeholders. This iterative process of monitoring and learning helps facilitate evidence-based decision-making and ensures that interventions are responsive to market needs.

Market facilitation approaches and techniques are essential for driving positive change within market systems. By adopting participatory approaches, value chain development, business development services, promoting innovation and adaptation, and engaging in continuous monitoring and learning, facilitators can effectively support market actors and create sustainable and inclusive market systems. These approaches and techniques enable market actors to navigate challenges, seize opportunities, and contribute to economic growth and poverty reduction.

Identifying and Analyzing Market Constraints

To effectively facilitate market development and drive positive change, it is crucial to identify and analyze the constraints that exist within a market system. Market constraints refer to the various factors that hinder the smooth functioning of markets and limit the potential of market actors. By understanding and addressing these constraints, market facilitators can create targeted interventions that address the root causes of market failures. In this article, we will explore the process of identifying and analyzing market constraints.

Conducting Market Assessments: The first step in identifying market constraints is to conduct comprehensive market assessments. This involves gathering relevant data and information about the market, including its structure, dynamics, and key actors. Market assessments may involve primary research, such as surveys and interviews with market actors, as well as secondary research, including analysis of market reports and studies. These assessments help facilitators gain a holistic understanding of the market and identify potential constraints.

Engaging with Market Actors: To gain deeper insights into market constraints, facilitators need to actively engage with market actors. This involves conducting consultations, focus group discussions, and stakeholder meetings to understand the perspectives and experiences of different actors. By involving market actors in the analysis process, facilitators can uncover hidden constraints and identify the underlying causes that impede market development.

Analyzing Market Systems: Market facilitators analyze the market system to identify the key constraints that are affecting its overall performance. This analysis involves examining the relationships, interactions, and interdependencies between different actors and components of the market system. By mapping out the value chain, identifying market functions, and assessing the enabling environment, facilitators can pinpoint the specific constraints that are hindering market development.

Applying Root Cause Analysis: Once the constraints are identified, facilitators apply root cause analysis to understand the underlying factors contributing to these constraints. This involves probing beyond the surface-level symptoms to identify the systemic issues that perpetuate market failures. By addressing the root causes, facilitators can design interventions that bring sustainable and long-term change to the market system.

Prioritizing Constraints: To allocate resources and plan interventions effectively, facilitators need to prioritize the identified constraints. This involves assessing the severity and impact of each constraint and considering the potential for intervention success. By prioritizing constraints, facilitators can focus their efforts on addressing the most critical issues and maximizing their impact on market development.

Identifying and analyzing market constraints is a vital step in market facilitation. By conducting market assessments, engaging with market actors, analyzing market systems, applying root cause analysis, and prioritizing constraints, facilitators can gain a comprehensive understanding of the challenges faced by market actors. This knowledge enables them to design targeted interventions that address the root causes of market failures and create sustainable change within market systems.

Chapter Two

Market Assessment and Analysis in MSD

Market assessment and analysis are critical components of Market Systems Development (MSD) initiatives. They provide valuable insights into the functioning of markets, identify constraints and opportunities, and inform the design of interventions to drive positive change. In this article, we will explore the importance of market assessment and analysis in MSD and discuss key approaches and tools used in this process.

Understanding Market Systems: Market assessment and analysis help practitioners gain a deep understanding of the dynamics and structure of the market systems they are working in. This includes mapping market actors, their relationships, and the flow of goods, services, and information within the market. By understanding the market system, practitioners can identify key bottlenecks, market failures, and opportunities for intervention.

Identifying Constraints and Opportunities: Market assessments enable practitioners to identify the constraints that limit the competitiveness and inclusivity of the market system. These constraints can range from policy and regulatory barriers to inadequate infrastructure, limited access to finance, or lack of skills and knowledge. Conversely, assessments also help identify potential opportunities for market development and growth. By understanding these constraints and opportunities, practitioners can design targeted interventions to address them effectively.

Stakeholder Engagement: Market assessment and analysis involve engaging with a wide range of stakeholders, including market actors, policymakers, and other relevant actors. This engagement facilitates the gathering of diverse perspectives, insights, and data necessary for a comprehensive understanding of the market system. It also helps build relationships and establish collaboration with stakeholders, fostering ownership and sustainability of interventions.

Tools and Approaches: Various tools and approaches can be used in market assessment and analysis, including market mapping, value chain analysis, SWOT analysis, and participatory methodologies such as focus group discussions and key informant interviews. These tools help gather qualitative and quantitative data, analyze market dynamics, and identify key issues and opportunities for intervention.

Data-Driven Decision Making: Market assessments provide practitioners with evidence-based information to make informed decisions about intervention strategies. By analyzing data and synthesizing findings, practitioners can prioritize interventions, allocate resources effectively, and monitor progress over time. This data-driven approach ensures that interventions are targeted, responsive, and adaptable to the evolving needs of the market system.

Market assessment and analysis are indispensable in the field of Market Systems Development. They provide practitioners with a comprehensive understanding of market systems, identify constraints and opportunities, engage stakeholders, and drive data-driven decision making. By conducting thorough assessments and using appropriate tools and approaches, practitioners can design and implement interventions that foster sustainable and inclusive market development.

Conducting a Market Assessment

A market assessment is a crucial step in understanding the dynamics, trends, and opportunities within a specific market. It helps businesses and organizations gain valuable insights into customer needs, competitor landscape, and market potential. In this article, we will explore the key steps involved in conducting a market assessment.

Define the Objective: The first step in conducting a market assessment is to clearly define the objective. What specific information are you seeking? Are you looking to enter a new market, launch a new product, or identify growth opportunities? By defining the objective, you can ensure that your assessment is focused and tailored to your needs.

Identify Target Market Segments: Next, identify the target market segments you want to assess. This involves segmenting the market based on factors such as demographics, psychographics, behavior, and geographic location. By understanding your target market segments, you can gather more relevant and targeted insights.

Gather Data: Collecting data is a critical part of the market assessment process. There are various sources of data that can be used, including primary research (surveys, interviews, focus groups) and secondary research (industry reports, market studies, government data). It is important to gather both qualitative and quantitative data to get a comprehensive understanding of the market.

Analyze Competitors: Analyzing competitors is an essential component of a market assessment. Identify and analyze your direct and indirect competitors, their strengths and weaknesses, market share, pricing strategies, and key differentiators. This analysis will help you identify opportunities to differentiate your product or service from the competition.

Assess Customer Needs: Understanding customer needs is crucial for success in any market. Conducting surveys or interviews with target customers can provide insights into their preferences, pain points, and purchasing behavior. By understanding customer needs, you can tailor your offerings to meet their expectations and gain a competitive advantage.

Evaluate Market Potential: Assessing the market potential involves analyzing the size of the market, its growth rate, and the demand for your product or service. This evaluation will help you understand the market's attractiveness and potential for growth.

Make Data-Driven Decisions: Finally, use the insights gathered from the market assessment to make data-driven decisions. This could involve refining your product or service offering, adjusting pricing strategies, identifying new target markets, or developing marketing campaigns that resonate with your target audience.

Conducting a market assessment is essential for businesses and organizations to gain a deeper understanding of their target market. By following these key steps and gathering relevant data, businesses can make informed decisions, identify growth opportunities, and develop effective strategies to succeed in the market.

Purpose and Objectives of Market Assessment

A market assessment serves as a valuable tool for businesses and organizations to gain a comprehensive understanding of a specific market. It involves evaluating various factors such as market size, customer needs, competitor landscape, and growth opportunities. The purpose of conducting a market assessment is to gather actionable insights that can inform strategic decision-making and drive business success. In this article, we will explore the key purposes and objectives of conducting a market assessment.

Identify Market Potential: One of the primary objectives of a market assessment is to determine the market potential. By analyzing market size, growth rate, and demand trends, businesses can assess the attractiveness of a market and identify opportunities for growth. Understanding the market potential helps businesses allocate resources effectively and make informed decisions regarding market entry or expansion.

Understand Customer Needs: Another important objective of a market assessment is to gain insights into customer needs and preferences. By conducting surveys, interviews, or focus groups, businesses can gather data on customer preferences, pain points, and purchasing behavior. Understanding customer needs enables businesses to develop products or services that align with customer expectations, leading to increased customer satisfaction and loyalty.

Analyze Competitor Landscape: A market assessment also aims to analyze the competitor landscape. By identifying and analyzing competitors, their strengths, weaknesses, and market share, businesses can gain a competitive advantage. This analysis helps businesses differentiate their offerings, identify market gaps, and develop effective strategies to outperform competitors.

Assess Market Risks and Challenges: Evaluating market risks and challenges is another objective of a market assessment. By understanding factors such as regulatory constraints, economic conditions, and technological advancements, businesses can anticipate potential obstacles and develop contingency plans. Assessing market risks helps businesses mitigate uncertainties and make informed decisions to navigate challenges effectively.

Support Strategic Decision-making: Ultimately, the purpose of a market assessment is to support strategic decision-making. By gathering relevant data and insights, businesses can make informed decisions regarding market entry, product development, pricing strategies, target audience selection, and marketing campaigns. The objective is to align business strategies with market realities and maximize the chances of success.

A Market assessment serves multiple purposes and objectives, all aimed at gaining a comprehensive understanding of a market. By conducting a thorough assessment, businesses can identify growth opportunities, understand customer needs, analyze competitors, assess market risks, and make informed strategic decisions. This enables businesses to stay competitive, drive growth, and achieve long-term success in the market.

Data Collection and Analysis Techniques

Data collection and analysis techniques are essential components of any research or analysis process. They enable businesses and organizations to gather and analyze relevant data to gain insights and make informed decisions. In this article, we will explore some commonly used data collection and analysis techniques.

Data Collection Techniques:

Surveys: Surveys involve collecting data from a sample of individuals through a set of structured questions. Surveys can be conducted online, via phone, or in-person. They are effective in gathering quantitative data and capturing a wide range of opinions and perspectives.

Interviews: Interviews involve conducting one-on-one or group discussions to collect qualitative data. Interviews provide an opportunity to delve deeper into a topic, understand motivations and experiences, and gather rich insights.

Observations: Observations involve systematically watching and documenting behaviors, interactions, and events. This technique is useful in capturing real-time data and understanding natural behavior in specific settings.

Focus Groups: Focus groups bring together a small group of individuals to discuss a particular topic. This technique allows for interactive discussions, encourages collaboration, and provides multiple perspectives on a given subject.

Data Analysis Techniques:

Descriptive Analysis: Descriptive analysis involves summarizing and describing the main characteristics of a dataset. This technique includes measures such as averages, frequencies, and percentages to provide a clear overview of the data.

Inferential Analysis: Inferential analysis involves drawing conclusions or making predictions about a larger population based on a sample of data. Techniques such as hypothesis testing, and regression analysis are commonly used for inferential analysis.

Qualitative Analysis: Qualitative analysis involves interpreting and making sense of non-numerical data, such as interview transcripts or open-ended survey responses. Techniques like thematic analysis or content analysis are used to identify patterns, themes, and insights.

Data Visualization: Data visualization techniques are used to present data in a visual format, such as charts, graphs, or info graphics. Data visualization helps in understanding complex data and communicating findings effectively.

Statistical Analysis: Statistical analysis involves applying statistical techniques to analyze data and identify relationships, patterns, or trends. Techniques like correlation analysis, chi-square tests, and ANOVA are commonly used in statistical analysis.

It is important to select the most appropriate data collection and analysis techniques based on the research objectives, available resources, and the type of data being collected. By employing these techniques effectively, businesses and organizations can gather valuable insights, make data-driven decisions, and drive success in their respective fields.

Identifying Market Opportunities and Challenges

The Market System Development (MSD) approach is a holistic and inclusive framework that aims to address market failures and promote sustainable economic growth in developing countries. Under this approach, identifying market opportunities and challenges is a crucial step in understanding the dynamics of a specific market system. Here, we will explore the importance of identifying market opportunities and challenges within the context of the MSD approach.

Understanding the Market System: The first step in identifying market opportunities and challenges is to gain a deep understanding of the market system. This involves analyzing the key actors, institutions, and relationships that shape the functioning of the market. By mapping the market system, stakeholders can identify gaps, inefficiencies, and potential areas for improvement.

Recognizing Market Opportunities: Identifying market opportunities requires identifying areas where there is potential for growth, innovation, and value creation. This can involve identifying underserved markets, unmet needs, or emerging trends. By recognizing market opportunities, stakeholders can develop interventions that promote inclusive and sustainable economic development.

Assessing Market Challenges: Market challenges can arise from a range of factors, such as limited access to finance, inadequate infrastructure, or weak institutions. It is important to identify these challenges to develop targeted interventions that address the root causes. By conducting a comprehensive analysis of market challenges, stakeholders can design strategies that mitigate risks and overcome barriers to market development.

Engaging Stakeholders: Identifying market opportunities and challenges requires active engagement with a wide range of stakeholders, including government agencies, private sector actors, civil society organizations, and local communities. By involving all relevant stakeholders, the MSD approach ensures that interventions are informed by diverse perspectives and are aligned with the needs and aspirations of the market system.

Promoting Systemic Change: The MSD approach goes beyond individual interventions and aims to promote systemic change within the market system. By identifying market opportunities and challenges, stakeholders can design interventions that address the underlying causes of market failures, rather than just treating the symptoms. This systemic approach helps to create sustainable and inclusive market systems that benefit all stakeholders.

Identifying market opportunities and challenges within the context of the MSD approach is essential for promoting inclusive and sustainable economic growth. By understanding the dynamics of the market system, recognizing opportunities, assessing challenges, engaging stakeholders, and promoting systemic change, the MSD approach enables stakeholders to develop targeted interventions that address the specific needs and constraints of the market. This comprehensive approach helps to unlock the potential of markets and create opportunities for economic empowerment and poverty reduction.

Market Mapping and Stakeholder Analysis

Market mapping and stakeholder analysis are crucial tools in understanding the dynamics of a market and the key actors involved. These processes provide valuable insights into the relationships, interests, and power dynamics within a market ecosystem. In this article, we will explore the importance of market mapping and stakeholder analysis and how they contribute to effective decision-making.

Market Mapping: Market mapping involves visualizing and analyzing the various components of a market, including products, services, competitors, suppliers, and customers. It helps identify the structure, size, and potential growth areas of the market. By mapping the market, businesses can make informed decisions regarding market entry, product positioning, and market segmentation. It also helps identify gaps and opportunities, allowing businesses to tailor their strategies to meet the needs of the market.

Stakeholder Analysis: Stakeholder analysis is a systematic process of identifying and understanding the individuals, groups, or organizations that have an interest or influence in a particular market. It helps businesses understand the motivations, expectations, and power dynamics of different stakeholders. By conducting stakeholder analysis, businesses can develop effective engagement strategies, anticipate potential conflicts or barriers, and build mutually beneficial relationships. It also enables businesses to identify strategic partners and leverage their expertise and resources for market success.

Identifying Key Players: Market mapping and stakeholder analysis help identify the key players within a market ecosystem. These players can include customers, suppliers, competitors, government agencies, industry associations, and non-governmental organizations. Understanding the roles and relationships of these key players is crucial for making strategic decisions and fostering collaborations. It allows businesses to identify potential partners, competitors, and influencers, enabling them to navigate the market landscape effectively.

Assessing Interests and Influences: Stakeholder analysis helps identify the interests, needs, and concerns of different stakeholders. It provides insights into their influence and decision-making power. By understanding the motivations and perspectives of stakeholders, businesses can tailor their strategies and communication approaches to address their interests and build trust. This enables businesses to build strong relationships, gain support, and effectively manage conflicts or challenges.

Enhancing Decision-Making: Market mapping and stakeholder analysis provide businesses with a comprehensive understanding of the market ecosystem. This knowledge enhances decision-making by enabling businesses to identify opportunities, anticipate risks, and develop strategies that align with the market dynamics. It allows businesses to make informed choices regarding market entry, product development, pricing, distribution, and marketing. By considering the diverse perspectives and interests of stakeholders, businesses can develop strategies that are socially responsible and sustainable in the long term.

Market mapping and stakeholder analysis are essential tools for understanding the complex dynamics of a market and its key players. By conducting market mapping, businesses can gain insights into the structure and growth potential of the market. Stakeholder analysis helps identify the interests, influences, and power dynamics of different stakeholders. Together, these processes equip businesses with the knowledge needed to make informed decisions, build strong relationships, and navigate the market ecosystem effectively. By utilizing market mapping and stakeholder analysis, businesses can enhance their competitiveness, foster collaborations, and contribute to sustainable market development.

Mapping Market Actors and Relationships

Mapping market actors and relationships is a crucial step in understanding the dynamics of a market and the complex web of interactions between different entities. This process involves identifying and analyzing the various actors involved in a market, including suppliers, customers, competitors, partners, and other stakeholders. By mapping these actors and their relationships, businesses can gain valuable insights into the structure, power dynamics, and opportunities within the market ecosystem. In this article, we will explore the importance of mapping market actors and relationships and how it contributes to effective decision-making.

Identifying Key Market Actors: Mapping market actors involves identifying and categorizing the key entities that play a significant role in a market. These can include suppliers, customers, distributors, retailers, industry influencers, and regulatory bodies. By understanding these actors, businesses can identify potential partners, competitors, and collaborators, allowing them to make informed decisions regarding market entry, product development, and distribution strategies.

Analyzing Relationships: Mapping market relationships involves analyzing the connections and interactions between various market actors. This includes understanding the nature of relationships, such as buyer-seller relationships, partnerships, and collaborations. By analyzing these relationships, businesses can identify patterns, dependencies, and potential areas for improvement. It also helps in identifying power dynamics and potential conflicts, allowing businesses to navigate the market ecosystem more effectively.

Understanding Power Dynamics: Mapping market actors and relationships provides insights into the power dynamics within a market. It helps identify the actors with significant influence and decision-making power. By understanding these power dynamics, businesses can develop strategies to engage and collaborate with influential actors to drive market success. It also helps businesses anticipate potential challenges and barriers to entry, allowing them to develop mitigation strategies accordingly.

Identifying Opportunities and Risks: Mapping market actors and relationships helps identify opportunities and potential risks within the market ecosystem. By analyzing the connections between actors, businesses can identify untapped market segments, potential partnerships, and emerging trends. Additionally, it helps identify potential risks, such as over-dependence on a single supplier or market saturation. This information allows businesses to develop strategies that leverage opportunities and mitigate risks effectively.

Enhancing Decision-Making: Mapping market actors and relationships enhances decision-making by providing a comprehensive understanding of the market ecosystem. It allows businesses to make informed choices regarding market entry, product positioning, pricing, distribution, and marketing strategies. By considering the relationships and power dynamics between actors, businesses can develop strategies that align with the market dynamics and foster mutually beneficial relationships.

Mapping market actors and relationships is a crucial step in understanding the dynamics of a market. By identifying key actors and analyzing their relationships, businesses can gain valuable insights into the structure, power dynamics, and opportunities within the market ecosystem. This knowledge enhances decision-making by allowing businesses to identify potential partners, competitors, and collaborators. It also helps in understanding power dynamics, anticipating risks, and leveraging opportunities effectively. By mapping market actors and relationships, businesses can navigate the market ecosystem more strategically, leading to increased competitiveness and long-term success.

Analyzing Stakeholder Interests and Influence

Analyzing stakeholder interests and influence is a crucial step in understanding the dynamics of a project or organization. Stakeholders are individuals or groups who have a vested interest in the outcome of a project or who are affected by its activities. They can include employees, customers, shareholders, suppliers, government agencies, and community members. By analyzing their interests and influence, businesses can make informed decisions, manage relationships, and ensure project success. In this article, we will explore the importance of analyzing stakeholder interests and influence and how it contributes to effective decision-making.

Identifying Stakeholders: The first step in analyzing stakeholder interests and influence is to identify all relevant stakeholders. This involves considering both internal and external entities that may have an impact on the project or organization. By identifying stakeholders, businesses can ensure that all perspectives and concerns are considered during the decision-making process.

Understanding Interests: Once stakeholders are identified, it is important to understand their interests. This includes determining what they hope to gain or achieve from the project or organization. Stakeholders may have financial, social, environmental, or strategic interests. By understanding these interests, businesses can align their decisions and actions to meet stakeholder expectations and needs.

Assessing Influence: Analyzing stakeholder influence involves understanding the power and ability of stakeholders to affect the project or organization. Some stakeholders may have more influence due to their position, resources, expertise, or relationships. By assessing influence, businesses can prioritize engagement efforts and allocate resources accordingly.

Managing Relationships: Analyzing stakeholder interests and influence helps in building and managing relationships effectively. By understanding stakeholders' interests, businesses can develop strategies to address concerns, communicate effectively, and build trust. By considering stakeholder influence, businesses can engage key stakeholders and involve them in decision-making processes, ensuring their buy-in and support.

Mitigating Risks: Analyzing stakeholder interests and influence also helps in identifying potential risks and challenges. By understanding stakeholders' interests, businesses can anticipate potential conflicts, resistance, or opposition. This allows them to develop mitigation strategies and proactive communication plans to address concerns and minimize negative impacts.

Enhancing Decision-Making: Analyzing stakeholder interests and influence enhances decision-making by considering a wider range of perspectives and potential impacts. By understanding stakeholders' interests, businesses can make decisions that balance their needs and expectations. By assessing stakeholder influence, businesses can navigate complex power dynamics and make decisions that are more likely to be accepted and supported.

Analyzing stakeholder interests and influence is essential for effective decision-making. By identifying stakeholders, understanding their interests, and assessing their influence, businesses can make informed decisions, manage relationships, and mitigate risks. It allows organizations to consider a broader range of perspectives, align decisions with stakeholder expectations, and build collaborative relationships. By analyzing stakeholder interests and influence, businesses can navigate complex environments and increase the likelihood of project success and long-term sustainability.

Engaging Key Stakeholders in MSD Interventions

Engaging key stakeholders is crucial for the success of any intervention, especially in the context of musculoskeletal disorders (MSDs). MSDs, which affect the muscles, bones, tendons, ligaments, and other parts of the body, can have a significant impact on individuals and workplaces. Engaging key stakeholders in MSD interventions ensures that their perspectives, expertise, and support are integrated into the planning, implementation, and evaluation processes. In this article, we will explore the importance of engaging key stakeholders in MSD interventions and how it contributes to a collaborative and effective approach.

Identifying Key Stakeholders: The first step in engaging key stakeholders is to identify the individuals or groups who have a vested interest in the intervention. This can include employees, managers, occupational health professionals, safety representatives, unions, and other relevant parties. By identifying key stakeholders, their unique perspectives and contributions can be recognized and utilized.

Building Relationships and Trust: Engaging key stakeholders requires building strong relationships and fostering trust. This involves open and transparent communication, active listening, and valuing their input. Building relationships and trust creates a supportive environment where stakeholders feel comfortable sharing their experiences, concerns, and ideas.

Involving Stakeholders in Decision-Making: Engaging key stakeholders means involving them in the decision-making process. This can include soliciting their input on intervention strategies, goal setting, and implementation plans. By involving stakeholders in decision-making, their expertise and insights can be utilized to ensure that interventions are tailored to their specific needs and circumstances.

Collaborative Problem-Solving: Engaging key stakeholders encourages collaborative problem-solving. By including stakeholders in discussions and brainstorming sessions, their diverse perspectives can contribute to innovative and effective solutions. Collaborative problem-solving promotes ownership of the intervention and increases the likelihood of successful outcomes.

Providing Education and Training: Engaging key stakeholders also involves providing education and training on MSD prevention and management. This ensures that stakeholders have the knowledge and skills to actively participate in the intervention and contribute to its success. Education and training can include workshops, seminars, and resources that empower stakeholders to take ownership of their health and safety.

Continuous Feedback and Evaluation: Engaging key stakeholders requires continuous feedback and evaluation mechanisms. This allows stakeholders to provide ongoing input, monitor progress, and identify areas for improvement. Continuous feedback and evaluation ensure that interventions remain responsive to changing needs and circumstances.

Engaging key stakeholders in MSD interventions is essential for a collaborative and effective approach. By identifying key stakeholders, building relationships and trust, involving stakeholders in decision-making, promoting collaborative problem-solving, providing education and training, and facilitating continuous feedback and evaluation, interventions can be tailored to the specific needs and circumstances of the stakeholders. Engaging key stakeholders ensures that their perspectives, expertise, and support are integrated into the intervention, increasing the likelihood of success and long-term sustainability.

Understanding Market Systems Dynamics

To thrive in today's dynamic and competitive business landscape, it is crucial to have a deep understanding of market systems dynamics. Market systems are complex networks of interactions between buyers, sellers, and other stakeholders that influence the flow of goods, services, and information. Understanding these dynamics is essential for businesses to make informed decisions, adapt to changing market conditions, and gain a competitive edge. In this article, we will explore the importance of understanding market systems dynamics and how it can contribute to business success.

Identifying Key Players and Relationships: Market systems involve a wide range of players, including suppliers, customers, competitors, and intermediaries. Understanding the relationships and interactions between these players is essential for businesses to identify opportunities, assess risks, and develop effective strategies. By recognizing the interdependencies and power dynamics within the market system, businesses can navigate the landscape more effectively.

Analyzing Supply and Demand Dynamics: Understanding the dynamics of supply and demand is crucial for businesses to optimize their production, pricing, and marketing strategies. By analyzing factors such as consumer preferences, competitor behavior, and market trends, businesses can anticipate changes in demand and adjust their offerings accordingly. This enables businesses to stay ahead of the competition and seize opportunities in the market.

Monitoring Market Trends and Forces: Market systems are influenced by various trends and forces, such as technological advancements, regulatory changes, and economic conditions. Businesses that proactively monitor and adapt to these trends can position themselves for success. By staying informed about market shifts and emerging opportunities, businesses can make timely adjustments to their strategies and stay ahead of the curve.

Building Strategic Partnerships: Understanding market systems dynamics can help businesses identify potential partners and build strategic alliances. Collaborating with complementary businesses can create synergies, expand market reach, and drive innovation. By leveraging the strengths and resources of their partners, businesses can achieve mutual growth and competitive advantage.

Anticipating and Managing Risks: Market systems are inherently dynamic and unpredictable, presenting both opportunities and risks. Businesses that understand the dynamics of the market system can anticipate and proactively manage risks. By conducting risk assessments, diversifying their customer base, and adapting their strategies to changing market conditions, businesses can mitigate potential challenges and maintain resilience.

Understanding market systems dynamics is vital for business success in today's fast-paced and competitive environment. By identifying key players and relationships, analyzing supply and demand dynamics, monitoring market trends and forces, building strategic partnerships, and anticipating and managing risks, businesses can navigate the complexities of the market system more effectively. A deep understanding of market systems dynamics empowers businesses to make informed decisions, seize opportunities, and stay ahead of the competition, ultimately leading to long-term success.

Feedback Loops and Interdependencies in Markets

In the world of economics and business, markets are not isolated entities. They are complex systems with feedback loops and interdependencies that play a crucial role in shaping their dynamics. Understanding these feedback loops and interdependencies is essential for businesses to navigate the intricacies of the market and make informed decisions. In this article, we will explore the concept of feedback loops, the interdependencies in markets, and their significance for businesses.

Feedback loops are cyclical processes in which the output of a system influences its own behavior. In the context of markets, feedback loops can have both positive (reinforcing) and negative (balancing) effects. Positive feedback loops amplify the effects of certain market factors, leading to self-reinforcing patterns. For example, when demand for a particular product increases, it leads to higher sales, which, in turn, attracts more suppliers. This creates a positive feedback loop that drives further growth in the market. On the other hand, negative feedback loops act as self-regulating mechanisms that counteract certain market factors. For instance, when prices of a product rise, it reduces demand, which then lowers prices. This creates a negative feedback loop that helps to stabilize the market.

Interdependencies in markets refer to the relationships and connections between different market players and factors. These interdependencies can be direct or indirect and can have a significant impact on the overall market dynamics. For example, the price of raw materials can have a direct impact on the production costs of manufacturers, which, in turn, affects the pricing of their products. Indirectly, changes in consumer preferences can influence the demand for products, which affects the revenue and profitability of businesses across the supply chain.

Understanding feedback loops and interdependencies in markets is crucial for businesses for several reasons. Firstly, it helps businesses anticipate and adapt to changes in the market. By recognizing the feedback loops at play, businesses can identify potential trends, opportunities, and risks. Secondly, it enables businesses to make informed decisions about pricing, production, and marketing strategies. Understanding the interdependencies in the market allows businesses to assess the potential impact of their decisions on other market players and factors. Lastly, it helps businesses to develop effective strategies for growth and sustainability. By leveraging the positive feedback loops and mitigating the negative ones, businesses can position themselves for long-term success.

Feedback loops and interdependencies are integral components of market dynamics. They shape the behavior and evolution of markets, influencing the decisions and outcomes of businesses. Understanding these complexities is essential for businesses to navigate the market effectively, make informed decisions, and adapt to changing conditions. By recognizing the feedback loops and interdependencies, businesses can leverage the opportunities and mitigate the risks presented by the market, ultimately leading to their success and growth.

Adapting to Change and Uncertainty in Market Systems

In the ever-evolving landscape of business and economics, one constant is change and uncertainty. Market systems are dynamic and subject to various external factors that can disrupt equilibrium and challenge the status quo. To thrive in such an environment, businesses must embrace adaptability and effectively navigate through change and uncertainty. In this article, we will explore the importance of adapting to change and uncertainty in market systems and provide strategies for businesses to stay resilient.

Change is an inevitable part of market systems. Factors such as technological advancements, shifting consumer preferences, economic fluctuations, and regulatory changes can significantly impact businesses. Companies that resist or fail to adapt to these changes run the risk of becoming obsolete or losing their competitive edge. Embracing change is crucial to stay relevant and seize opportunities that arise from evolving market conditions.

Uncertainty is another inherent aspect of market systems. External factors such as geopolitical events, natural disasters, and economic downturns can create a sense of volatility and unpredictability. Businesses that can effectively manage uncertainty are better equipped to weather storms and emerge stronger. By developing contingency plans, diversifying revenue streams, and staying agile, businesses can mitigate the impact of uncertainty and position themselves for success.

To adapt to change and uncertainty, businesses must adopt a proactive mindset. This involves monitoring market trends, gathering insights, and staying informed about industry developments. By anticipating potential changes and disruptions, businesses can take early action and adjust their strategies accordingly. Additionally, fostering a culture of innovation and continuous learning within the organization can enable businesses to adapt quickly and seize opportunities.

Flexibility is also crucial in adapting to change and uncertainty. Businesses should be open to exploring new markets, diversifying their product offerings, and embracing emerging technologies. By being flexible and open-minded, businesses can capitalize on emerging trends and gain a competitive advantage.

Furthermore, building strong partnerships and collaborations can enhance adaptability. By forming strategic alliances and networks, businesses can leverage the expertise and resources of others to navigate through change and uncertainty. Collaborative efforts can lead to innovative solutions and shared knowledge, strengthening the overall resilience of the market system.

Adapting to change and uncertainty is essential for success in market systems. By embracing change, managing uncertainty, and fostering a proactive and flexible mindset, businesses can position themselves to thrive in dynamic environments. It is through adaptability that businesses can seize opportunities, mitigate risks, and stay ahead of the competition. As market systems continue to evolve, those who are resilient and adaptable will be best equipped to navigate the ever-changing landscape and emerge as leaders in their respective industries.

Assessing Market System Resilience and Sustainability

In a rapidly changing and interconnected world, assessing the resilience and sustainability of market systems has become crucial for businesses and policymakers alike. Market systems operate within complex economic, social, and environmental contexts, and understanding their ability to adapt, withstand shocks, and maintain long-term viability is essential. In this article, we will explore the importance of assessing market system resilience and sustainability and discuss key factors to consider in the evaluation process.

Market system resilience refers to the system's capacity to absorb and recover from shocks or disturbances without losing its fundamental structure or function. It involves the ability to adapt, innovate, and bounce back in the face of challenges. Assessing resilience helps businesses identify vulnerabilities, anticipate potential risks, and develop strategies to mitigate them. It allows policymakers to design policies and interventions that promote stability and mitigate the negative impacts of disruptions.

Market system sustainability, on the other hand, focuses on the long-term viability and endurance of the system. It considers the economic, social, and environmental dimensions of sustainability. Assessing sustainability helps businesses and policymakers evaluate the system's ability to meet present needs without compromising the ability of future generations to meet their own needs. It involves analyzing factors such as resource efficiency, social equity, and environmental impact.

In assessing market system resilience and sustainability, several key factors should be considered. These include:

Diversity and Redundancy: The presence of diverse actors, products, and markets can enhance resilience by reducing dependence on a single source. Redundancy ensures there are alternative pathways and resources available in the event of disruptions.

Adaptive Capacity: The ability of the system to learn, innovate, and adapt in response to changing conditions is crucial for long-term sustainability. This includes the capacity to adjust strategies, technologies, and business models.

Social Cohesion: A market system that fosters social cohesion and inclusivity is more likely to be resilient and sustainable. It involves promoting fair trade practices, labor rights, and equitable access to resources and opportunities.

Environmental Stewardship: Assessing the environmental impact of market systems is vital for sustainability. This includes evaluating resource consumption, waste generation, and the system's contribution to climate change and biodiversity loss.

Governance and Institutions: Effective governance structures and institutions that promote transparency, accountability, and the rule of law are essential for resilient and sustainable market systems.

By assessing market system resilience and sustainability, businesses and policymakers can identify areas for improvement, implement targeted interventions, and ensure long-term success. It enables them to navigate uncertainties, mitigate risks, and contribute to a more resilient and sustainable economy. As market systems continue to evolve, the ability to assess and enhance resilience and sustainability will be crucial for maintaining competitive advantage and creating a prosperous future for all.

Chapter Three

Market Transformation

Market transformation refers to the process of driving significant and sustainable change within a specific industry or market sector. It involves shifting market dynamics, practices, and behaviors to align with broader social, economic, and environmental goals. Market transformation strategies play a vital role in accelerating the transition towards more sustainable and responsible business practices. In this article, we will explore key strategies for market transformation and their potential impact.

Strategies for Market Transformation

Education and Awareness: One of the foundational strategies for market transformation is educating and raising awareness among stakeholders about the benefits of sustainable practices. This includes providing information, training, and resources to businesses, consumers, and policymakers to foster a deeper understanding of the social and environmental impacts of their choices.

Regulatory and Policy Interventions: Governments, through regulatory and policy interventions, can drive market transformation by setting standards, mandates, and incentives that push businesses towards sustainable practices. This can include regulations on emissions, waste management, and product labeling, as well as financial incentives for adopting sustainable technologies and practices.

Collaboration and Partnerships: Market transformation often requires collaboration and partnerships between different stakeholders, including businesses, governments, NGOs, and consumers. By working together, these actors can leverage their resources, knowledge, and influence to drive change collectively. Collaborative initiatives can focus on research and development, sharing best practices, and advocating for policy changes.

Market-Based Instruments: Market-based instruments, such as carbon pricing or emissions trading schemes, can create economic incentives for businesses to adopt sustainable practices. These instruments internalize the costs of environmental and social externalities, encouraging businesses to reduce their negative impacts and invest in sustainable solutions.

Innovation and Technology: Embracing innovation and technology is crucial for market transformation. New technologies, such as renewable energy, circular economy solutions, and sustainable materials, can disrupt traditional market practices and catalyze sustainable change. Encouraging research and development, supporting startups, and fostering a culture of innovation can drive transformation within industries.

Consumer Demand and Behavior Change: Ultimately, market transformation relies on consumer demand and behavior change. By empowering consumers with information, promoting sustainable purchasing choices, and encouraging responsible consumption, businesses can respond to shifting market demands and drive transformation from the bottom-up.

By employing these strategies, market transformation can be achieved, leading to a more sustainable and responsible economy. It requires the collective effort of businesses, governments, NGOs, and consumers to create a conducive environment for change. Market transformation not only benefits the environment and society but also offers new business opportunities, enhanced competitiveness, and long-term success for those who embrace it.

Promoting inclusive growth in Market Systems

Inclusive growth is a concept that aims to ensure that the benefits of economic development are shared equitably across all segments of society, including marginalized and vulnerable populations. In the context of market systems, promoting inclusive growth involves creating an enabling environment that allows all participants, regardless of their socio-economic status, to access and benefit from market opportunities. In this article, we will explore strategies and approaches to promote inclusive growth in market systems.

Increasing Access to Markets: One of the key elements of promoting inclusive growth is to ensure that all individuals, particularly those in marginalized communities, have access to markets. This can be achieved by improving physical infrastructure, such as roads and transportation networks, to connect remote areas to markets. Additionally, providing financial services, such as microcredit and savings accounts, can enable individuals to participate in economic activities and access market opportunities.

Supporting Small and Medium Enterprises (SMEs): SMEs are often the backbone of local economies and can play a crucial role in inclusive growth. Supporting SMEs through capacity building programs, access to finance, and technical assistance can help them overcome barriers and thrive in competitive markets. Furthermore, promoting entrepreneurship and providing mentorship opportunities can empower individuals from marginalized communities to start and grow their businesses.

Enhancing Skills and Education: Investing in education and skills development is vital for promoting inclusive growth. By providing quality education and training programs, individuals can acquire the necessary knowledge and skills to participate in the market economy. This includes both technical skills, such as vocational training, as well as soft skills like critical thinking and communication.

Addressing Social and Gender Inequalities: Inclusive growth requires addressing social and gender inequalities that hinder the participation of certain groups in market systems. This can be achieved through policy interventions that promote equal opportunities, affirmative action measures, and initiatives to empower women and other marginalized groups. Ensuring that laws and regulations protect the rights of all individuals, regardless of their background, is also crucial.

Promoting Collaboration and Partnerships: Promoting inclusive growth in market systems requires collaboration between various stakeholders, including governments, civil society organizations, private sector actors, and development agencies. Building partnerships can facilitate knowledge sharing, resource mobilization, and coordination of efforts to implement inclusive growth strategies.

Promoting inclusive growth in market systems is not only a moral imperative but also contributes to sustainable and resilient economies. By creating an enabling environment that fosters equal opportunities, access, and participation, we can build more inclusive societies and unlock the potential of all individuals, ultimately leading to shared prosperity and sustainable development.

Addressing Gender and Social Inequalities

Gender and social inequalities are pervasive issues that hinder the progress and development of societies worldwide. The unequal distribution of resources, opportunities, and power based on gender, race, ethnicity, or socioeconomic status creates barriers for marginalized individuals and perpetuates systemic discrimination. In this article, we will explore the importance of addressing gender and social inequalities and discuss strategies to promote equality and inclusivity.

Education and Awareness: Education plays a vital role in challenging gender and social inequalities. By promoting inclusive and equitable education systems, we can empower individuals to challenge stereotypes, biases, and discriminatory practices. It is crucial to educate both children and adults about gender equality, human rights, and the value of diversity. Public awareness campaigns, workshops, and training programs can help foster a more inclusive and accepting society.

Policy and Legal Reforms: Governments and policymakers have a significant role to play in addressing gender and social inequalities. Implementing and enforcing laws that protect the rights of marginalized individuals, such as anti-discrimination laws and equal pay legislation, is essential. Policies that promote gender mainstreaming and social inclusion can help level the playing field and create a more equitable society.

Empowering Marginalized Communities: Empowering marginalized communities through targeted interventions and support is crucial for addressing inequalities. This includes providing access to healthcare, economic opportunities, and social protection programs. Initiatives that promote entrepreneurship, skill development, and financial inclusion can help individuals from marginalized backgrounds gain economic independence and break the cycle of poverty.

Promoting Gender Equality in the Workplace: Gender inequality in the workplace remains a significant challenge. Employers can take proactive steps to promote diversity and inclusion by implementing policies and practices that ensure equal opportunities, pay equity, and a safe working environment. Addressing unconscious biases, providing mentorship programs, and promoting work-life balance are crucial steps towards achieving gender equality in the workplace.

Collaboration and Partnerships: Addressing gender and social inequalities requires collective efforts from all stakeholders, including governments, civil society organizations, and the private sector. Collaborative partnerships can help share best practices, resources, and expertise to address complex social issues effectively. Engaging men and boys as allies in the fight for gender equality is also crucial to challenge patriarchal norms and promote inclusivity.

Addressing gender and social inequalities is not only a matter of social justice but also a prerequisite for sustainable development and economic growth. By creating a more inclusive and equitable society, we can unlock the full potential of individuals, foster innovation, and build resilient communities. It is our collective responsibility to challenge discriminatory practices, dismantle systemic barriers, and work towards a future where everyone can thrive, regardless of their gender or social background.

Reaching Marginalized and Vulnerable Groups

Reaching marginalized and vulnerable groups is a critical aspect of promoting inclusivity, equality, and social justice. These groups, which can include individuals facing poverty, discrimination, disability, or social exclusion, often face significant barriers in accessing essential services and opportunities. In this article, we will explore the importance of reaching marginalized and vulnerable groups and discuss strategies to ensure their inclusion and empowerment.

Identifying Barriers: The first step in reaching marginalized and vulnerable groups is to understand the specific barriers they face. These barriers can be economic, social, cultural, or institutional in nature. Conducting comprehensive research, engaging with community members, and consulting with relevant stakeholders are crucial in identifying and addressing these barriers effectively.

Tailored Approaches: One size does not fit all when it comes to reaching marginalized and vulnerable groups. It is important to develop tailored approaches and interventions that address the unique needs and challenges faced by these groups. This can involve adapting service delivery methods, providing language or cultural support, and incorporating participatory approaches to ensure their voices are heard and their perspectives are considered.

Building Trust and Relationships: Building trust and relationships with marginalized and vulnerable groups is essential for effective outreach. This can be achieved by engaging community leaders, local organizations, and trusted individuals who can act as intermediaries. Creating safe and inclusive spaces for dialogue and collaboration can help foster trust and ensure that the needs and concerns of these groups are heard and addressed.

Accessible Services and Infrastructure: Ensuring that services and infrastructure are accessible to marginalized and vulnerable groups is crucial. This can involve removing physical barriers, providing transportation options, and making information available in multiple formats or languages. It is important to consider the specific needs and limitations of these groups to ensure that they can fully participate and benefit from the services being provided.

Empowering and Building Capacities: Empowering marginalized and vulnerable groups is key to sustainable change. This can involve providing skills training, education, and resources that enable individuals to improve their socio-economic status and advocate for their rights. Creating opportunities for leadership and meaningful participation can also help build the capacities of these groups to actively engage in decision-making processes.

Reaching marginalized and vulnerable groups requires a holistic and multi-faceted approach that addresses the systemic issues they face. By actively listening, involving them in the process, and providing tailored support, we can ensure their inclusion and empower them to overcome barriers and achieve their full potential. The concerted efforts of governments, civil society organizations, and communities are essential to create a more equitable and inclusive society for all.

Enhancing Access to Opportunities for All

Ensuring equal access to opportunities for all individuals is crucial for promoting social equity and fostering inclusive societies. However, many people face barriers that prevent them from fully participating in social, economic, and educational opportunities. In this article, we will discuss the importance of enhancing access to opportunities for all and explore strategies to achieve this goal.

Identifying Barriers: The first step in enhancing access to opportunities for all is to identify the barriers that individuals face. These barriers can be structural, such as discrimination, lack of inclusive policies, or inadequate infrastructure. By conducting thorough research and engaging with affected communities, we can gain insights into the specific challenges they face and develop targeted solutions.

Inclusive Policies and Legislation: Creating inclusive policies and legislation is essential for breaking down barriers and ensuring equal access to opportunities. Governments and organizations should prioritize the development and implementation of policies that address discrimination, promote diversity, and provide equal access to education, employment, healthcare, and other essential services.

Education and Skills Development: Education plays a pivotal role in enhancing access to opportunities. By providing quality education and skills development programs, individuals can acquire the knowledge and skills needed to pursue their desired paths. It is crucial to ensure that education is accessible and inclusive, addressing the needs of diverse learners and removing barriers to participation.

Empowering Marginalized Communities: Empowering marginalized communities is key to enhancing access to opportunities. This can involve providing support, resources, and training to individuals from disadvantaged backgrounds. By promoting entrepreneurship, vocational training, and mentorship programs, we can empower individuals to create their own opportunities and overcome systemic barriers.

Collaboration and Partnerships: Achieving equal access to opportunities requires collaboration among various stakeholders, including governments, civil society organizations, and the private sector. By working together, we can leverage resources, knowledge, and expertise to develop comprehensive strategies and initiatives that address the diverse needs of individuals and communities.

Enhancing access to opportunities for all is a fundamental aspect of promoting social justice and equality. By identifying barriers, implementing inclusive policies, investing in education and skills development, empowering marginalized communities, and fostering collaboration, we can create a more inclusive and equitable society where everyone has the chance to thrive and reach their full potential.

Sustainable Business Development and Environmental Considerations

In today's rapidly changing world, businesses are increasingly recognizing the importance of sustainable development and environmental considerations. Sustainable business practices not only benefit the environment but also contribute to long-term profitability, brand reputation, and social responsibility. In this article, we will discuss the significance of sustainable business development and the integration of environmental considerations.

Environmental Impact Assessment: One of the first steps in sustainable business development is to conduct a thorough environmental impact assessment. This involves evaluating the potential environmental effects of business operations and identifying ways to minimize negative impacts. By assessing factors such as resource consumption, waste generation, and emissions, businesses can identify opportunities for improvement and implement sustainable practices.

Resource Efficiency: Sustainable business development entails optimizing resource use and minimizing waste. By adopting energy-efficient technologies, implementing recycling programs, and reducing water consumption, businesses can decrease their environmental footprint while also cutting costs. Resource efficiency measures can range from simple changes, such as switching to energy-saving light bulbs, to more complex initiatives like implementing renewable energy systems.

Supply Chain Management: Businesses should consider the environmental impact of their supply chains. This involves evaluating suppliers' sustainability practices, promoting responsible sourcing, and reducing transportation emissions. By partnering with suppliers that prioritize sustainable practices, businesses can contribute to a more sustainable and resilient supply chain.

Stakeholder Engagement: Engaging stakeholders, including employees, customers, and local communities, is essential in sustainable business development. By involving stakeholders in decision-making processes, businesses can gain valuable insights and build trust. Engaging employees in sustainability initiatives can also foster a sense of purpose and commitment.

Corporate Social Responsibility: Businesses should embrace corporate social responsibility (CSR) as an integral part of their operations. This entails taking responsibility for the social, economic, and environmental impacts of their activities. By investing in community development, supporting environmental initiatives, and promoting ethical business practices, businesses can enhance their reputation and contribute to sustainable development.

Sustainable business development and environmental considerations are crucial for long-term success. By conducting environmental impact assessments, optimizing resource efficiency, managing supply chains, engaging stakeholders, and embracing corporate social responsibility, businesses can make a positive impact on the environment while also reaping the benefits of sustainable practices. As businesses strive to grow and succeed, it is imperative to prioritize sustainability and contribute to a greener and more sustainable future.

Integrating Environmental Sustainability in Market Systems

The concept of environmental sustainability has gained significant attention in recent years, and businesses are increasingly recognizing the need to integrate sustainability into their market systems. This involves incorporating environmental considerations into various aspects of business operations, including production processes, supply chains, and marketing strategies. In this article, we will explore the importance of integrating environmental sustainability in market systems and the benefits it brings to businesses.

Sustainable Production Practices: One of the key aspects of integrating environmental sustainability in market systems is adopting sustainable production practices. This involves minimizing resource consumption, reducing waste generation, and incorporating renewable energy sources. By implementing energy-efficient technologies, optimizing production processes, and reducing emissions, businesses can reduce their environmental impact while maintaining profitability.

Sustainable Supply Chains: Another crucial element of integrating environmental sustainability is ensuring sustainability throughout the supply chain. This involves selecting suppliers that prioritize sustainability, promoting responsible sourcing, and minimizing transportation emissions. By working with environmentally conscious suppliers and implementing sustainable procurement practices, businesses can contribute to a more sustainable and resilient supply chain.

Eco-friendly Products and Services: Integrating environmental sustainability in market systems also entails offering eco-friendly products and services. This involves developing materials andoduct designs, using environmentally friendly materials, and promoting recycling and reuse. By offering sustainable alternatives to customers, businesses can tap into the growing demand for environmentally conscious products and attract a wider customer base.

Green Marketing Strategies: Businesses can also integrate environmental sustainability in their marketing strategies. This involves promoting the environmental benefits of their products or services, highlighting sustainable practices in their advertising, and engaging in cause marketing initiatives. By aligning their marketing efforts with environmental sustainability, businesses can enhance their brand reputation and appeal to environmentally conscious consumers.

Long-term Benefits: Integrating environmental sustainability in market systems offers several long-term benefits for businesses. Firstly, it helps businesses stay ahead of regulations and compliance requirements related to environmental issues. Secondly, it enhances brand reputation and customer loyalty, as consumers are increasingly favoring sustainable businesses. Finally, it fosters innovation and encourages businesses to find creative solutions to environmental challenges, leading to long-term competitive advantage.

Integrating environmental sustainability in market systems is crucial for businesses to thrive in a rapidly changing world. By adopting sustainable production practices, ensuring sustainability throughout the supply chain, offering eco-friendly products and services, and implementing green marketing strategies, businesses can contribute to a more sustainable future while reaping the benefits of increased customer loyalty and long-term profitability. Embracing environmental sustainability is not only a responsibility but also an opportunity for businesses to make a positive impact on the planet and secure their position in the market.

Promoting Climate Resilience and Green Technologies

In the face of climate change and its far-reaching impacts, promoting climate resilience and green technologies has become an urgent global priority. The concept of climate resilience refers to the ability of communities, ecosystems, and economies to adapt and withstand the impacts of climate change. Green technologies, on the other hand, encompass a wide range of innovative solutions that are environmentally friendly and help reduce greenhouse gas emissions. In this article, we will delve into the importance of promoting climate resilience and green technologies in the context of sustainable development.

Climate Resilience: Climate resilience is crucial for communities, particularly those in vulnerable regions, to adapt and respond effectively to the challenges posed by climate change. Promoting climate resilience involves implementing measures such as building infrastructure that can withstand extreme weather events, developing early warning systems, and enhancing disaster preparedness. By investing in climate resilience, communities can reduce the risk of climate-related disasters, protect livelihoods, and ensure the long-term sustainability of their socio-economic systems.

Green Technologies: Green technologies play a vital role in mitigating climate change by reducing greenhouse gas emissions and promoting sustainable practices. These technologies encompass a wide range of innovations, including renewable energy sources, energy-efficient systems, sustainable agriculture practices, waste management solutions, and smart city initiatives. By promoting the adoption of green technologies, societies can transition to a low-carbon economy, reduce their ecological footprint, and achieve sustainable development goals.

Benefits of Promoting Climate Resilience and Green Technologies: The promotion of climate resilience and green technologies offers numerous benefits. Firstly, it helps reduce greenhouse gas emissions and combat climate change, leading to a healthier planet for future generations. Secondly, it fosters economic growth and job creation, as the development and implementation of green technologies require skilled professionals and innovative businesses. Additionally, it enhances energy security by reducing dependence on fossil fuels and promoting the use of renewable energy sources. Moreover, promoting climate resilience and green technologies can improve public health by reducing pollution and mitigating the impacts of climate-related health risks.

International Cooperation: Promoting climate resilience and green technologies requires international cooperation and collaboration. Governments, private sector entities, civil society organizations, and international institutions need to work together to develop policies, provide financial support, and share knowledge and best practices. International agreements, such as the Paris Agreement, provide a framework for countries to collaborate in addressing climate change and promoting sustainable development.

Promoting climate resilience and green technologies is essential for achieving sustainable development and mitigating the impacts of climate change. By investing in climate resilience measures and adopting green technologies, communities can adapt to changing environmental conditions, reduce greenhouse gas emissions, and foster economic growth. Furthermore, international cooperation is vital in driving the adoption and implementation of climate-resilient practices and green technologies. As we face the challenges of climate change, it is imperative that we prioritize and promote climate resilience and green technologies as integral components of a sustainable future.

Balancing Economic Growth with Environmental Conservation

In today's world, the pursuit of economic growth often comes at the expense of environmental conservation. However, achieving a harmonious balance between economic development and environmental protection is crucial for sustainable development. In this article, we will explore the importance of balancing economic growth with environmental conservation in the context of sustainable development.

Sustainable Development: Sustainable development seeks to meet the needs of the present without compromising the ability of future generations to meet their own needs. It requires a balanced approach that takes into account social, economic, and environmental factors. Balancing economic growth with environmental conservation is a fundamental aspect of sustainable development, as it ensures the long-term well-being of both people and the planet.

Environmental Conservation: Environmental conservation involves the protection and preservation of natural resources, ecosystems, and biodiversity. It encompasses activities such as habitat restoration, wildlife conservation, sustainable land use, and responsible waste management. By conserving the environment, we can maintain the ecological balance, protect vulnerable species, and safeguard the planet's natural beauty for future generations.

Economic Growth: Economic growth, on the other hand, refers to an increase in the production and consumption of goods and services within an economy. While economic growth is essential for poverty reduction, job creation, and improving living standards, it often leads to negative environmental impacts. These include deforestation, pollution, depletion of natural resources, and increased greenhouse gas emissions.

Importance of Balance: Balancing economic growth with environmental conservation is crucial for several reasons. Firstly, a healthy environment is necessary for human well-being and quality of life. Clean air, access to safe water, and a diverse ecosystem are all essential for our health and happiness. Secondly, environmental degradation can have severe economic consequences, such as loss of biodiversity, reduced agricultural productivity, and increased costs due to pollution and climate change. Lastly, achieving sustainable development requires a long-term perspective that considers the needs of future generations. By balancing economic growth with environmental conservation, we ensure that resources are used responsibly, and that the planet can sustainably support future generations.

Strategies for Balancing Economic Growth and Environmental Conservation: Achieving a balance between economic growth and environmental conservation requires a multi-faceted approach. This includes implementing sustainable practices in industries such as energy, agriculture, and manufacturing, promoting renewable energy sources, encouraging responsible consumption and production patterns, and investing in green technologies and innovation. Additionally, effective environmental policies, regulations, and international cooperation are essential for ensuring that economic development occurs within the bounds of environmental sustainability.

Balancing economic growth with environmental conservation is vital for sustainable development. It requires a holistic approach that considers social, economic, and environmental factors. By promoting sustainable practices, investing in green technologies, and implementing effective environmental policies, we can achieve a harmonious balance between economic growth and environmental conservation. This will not only ensure a prosperous future for humanity but also preserve the planet's natural resources and ecosystems for generations to come.

Leveraging Technology and Innovation in MSD

In the field of sustainable development, leveraging technology and innovation is crucial for driving progress and finding solutions to complex challenges. Technology has the potential to revolutionize the way we approach sustainable development, making it more efficient, effective, and scalable. In this article, we will explore the importance of leveraging technology and innovation in the context of MSD

Enhancing Efficiency: Technology and innovation can significantly improve the efficiency of MSD initiatives. By leveraging digital platforms, data analytics, and automation, organizations can streamline processes, reduce costs, and optimize resource allocation. For example, the use of mobile applications and cloud-based systems can facilitate real-time data collection, monitoring, and evaluation of development projects. This enables stakeholders to make informed decisions and take timely action to achieve the desired outcomes.

Scaling Impact: Technology and innovation have the power to scale the impact of MSD efforts. Using digital platforms, social media, and online communication tools, organizations can reach a larger audience, raise awareness, and mobilize resources more effectively. Furthermore, innovative solutions such as renewable energy technologies, clean water purification systems, and low-cost healthcare devices can be replicated and deployed in different regions, accelerating progress towards the MSD goals.

Promoting Inclusivity: Technology and innovation can also play a vital role in promoting inclusivity in MSD. They can bridge the digital divide, empower marginalized communities, and provide access to essential services and information. For instance, mobile banking and digital payment systems enable financial inclusion, allowing individuals in remote areas to access banking services and make transactions. Similarly, e-learning platforms and digital literacy initiatives can provide education and skill development opportunities to underserved populations.

Fostering Collaboration: Technology and innovation foster collaboration among various stakeholders involved in MSD. Through digital platforms and online collaboration tools, organizations, governments, and communities can share knowledge, exchange best practices, and collectively work towards achieving the MSD goals. This collaboration enhances coordination, reduces duplication of efforts, and promotes synergy among different actors.

Addressing Emerging Challenges: Technology and innovation are essential in addressing emerging challenges in the field of sustainable development. For example, the use of artificial intelligence (AI) and machine learning can help in analyzing complex data sets, predicting trends, and identifying potential risks. This can aid in early warning systems for natural disasters, disease outbreaks, and climate change impacts, enabling proactive measures to be taken.

Leveraging technology and innovation is crucial in advancing MSD. By enhancing efficiency, scaling impact, promoting inclusivity, fostering collaboration, and addressing emerging challenges, technology can propel us towards achieving the Millennium Development Goals. However, it is essential to ensure that technology is accessible, affordable, and ethically deployed to avoid exacerbating existing inequalities. By harnessing the power of technology and innovation, we can accelerate progress towards a more sustainable and equitable future.

Digital Transformation and Market Systems

Digital transformation is revolutionizing various industries, including the field of sustainable development. In the context of Market Systems Development (MSD), digital transformation plays a crucial role in driving innovation, efficiency, and inclusivity. It enables the integration of technology into market systems, leading to improved outcomes and sustainable development. In this article, we will explore the significance of digital transformation in MSD and its impact on market systems.

Enhancing Efficiency: Digital transformation in MSD streamlines processes and improves efficiency in market systems. Using digital platforms, automation, and data analytics, organizations can optimize supply chains, reduce transaction costs, and improve resource allocation. For example, digital marketplaces and e-commerce platforms facilitate faster and more transparent transactions, connecting buyers and sellers efficiently. This leads to increased productivity, reduced waste, and improved market functioning.

Enabling Inclusive Market Systems: Digital transformation promotes inclusivity by expanding access to markets for marginalized and underserved populations. Mobile technologies and digital payment systems, for instance, enable small-scale farmers and entrepreneurs in remote areas to participate in formal markets. This increases their income opportunities and improves their livelihoods. Moreover, digital platforms can provide market information, training, and support to empower marginalized groups and promote their inclusion in market systems.

Facilitating Data-Driven Decision-Making: Digital transformation enables the collection, analysis, and utilization of vast amounts of data. This data-driven approach enhances decision-making in MSD by providing valuable insights into market dynamics, consumer behavior, and economic trends. By leveraging data analytics and business intelligence tools, organizations can make informed decisions, develop targeted interventions, and monitor the impact of their initiatives. This leads to more effective and evidence-based strategies for sustainable development.

Fostering Innovation and Collaboration: Digital transformation fosters innovation and collaboration within market systems. It encourages the emergence of new business models, products, and services that address social and environmental challenges. Through digital platforms and online communities, stakeholders can collaborate, share knowledge, and co-create solutions. This collaboration promotes learning, creativity, and the exchange of best practices, leading to continuous improvement and adaptation within market systems.

Building Resilient Market Systems: Digital transformation strengthens the resilience of market systems in the face of disruptions and crises. By embracing digital technologies, organizations can diversify their supply chains, adapt to changing market conditions, and mitigate risks. For example, e-commerce and online marketplaces enable businesses to reach customers even during periods of lockdown or travel restrictions. This resilience ensures the continuity of economic activities and sustains livelihoods, even in challenging circumstances.

Digital transformation is a game-changer in MSD, revolutionizing market systems and driving sustainable development. By enhancing efficiency, promoting inclusivity, facilitating data-driven decision-making, fostering innovation and collaboration, and building resilient market systems, digital transformation empowers stakeholders to create positive and lasting impact. However, it is essential to ensure equitable access to digital technologies, address digital literacy gaps, and consider the ethical implications of digital transformation in order to maximize its benefits for all. Through the integration of digital technologies into market systems, we can accelerate progress towards achieving sustainable development goals and creating a more inclusive and prosperous future.

Harnessing Mobile Technology and E-commerce

Mobile technology and e-commerce have revolutionized the way businesses operate and interact with customers. Harnessing the power of mobile technology and e-commerce is crucial for businesses to stay competitive and provide seamless and convenient services to their customers.

Importance of Mobile Technology in MSD

Mobile technology plays a pivotal role in MSD by enabling businesses to connect with customers anytime, anywhere. With the increasing popularity of smartphones and mobile apps, businesses can leverage mobile technology to streamline service delivery processes, enhance customer experiences, and drive customer loyalty. Mobile technology allows businesses to offer services such as mobile ordering, tracking, and real-time updates, which significantly improve convenience and efficiency for customers.

Leveraging E-commerce in MSD

E-commerce has transformed the way businesses sell products and services, and it has a significant impact on MSD. By integrating e-commerce platforms into their operations, businesses can reach a wider customer base, increase sales, and provide a seamless buying experience. E-commerce platforms enable businesses to showcase their products or services, accept online payments, and provide personalized recommendations to customers. This not only enhances the customer experience but also allows businesses to gather valuable customer data for targeted marketing and improved service offerings.

Benefits of Harnessing Mobile Technology and E-commerce in MSD

Enhanced Convenience: Mobile technology and e-commerce enable customers to access services and make purchases at their convenience, eliminating the need for physical visits or phone calls.

Improved Efficiency: By digitizing processes and automating tasks, businesses can streamline operations, reduce manual errors, and provide faster service delivery.

Personalized Experiences: Mobile technology and e-commerce platforms allow businesses to gather customer data and provide personalized recommendations and offers tailored to individual preferences, fostering customer loyalty.

Increased Reach: Mobile technology and e-commerce platforms give businesses the opportunity to reach a wider audience, including customers in remote areas or those who prefer online interactions.

Data-driven Decision Making: By leveraging mobile technology and e-commerce, businesses can gather and analyze customer data to make informed decisions, optimize service offerings, and target marketing efforts effectively.

Competitive Advantage: Businesses that harness mobile technology and e-commerce in MSD gain a competitive edge by providing convenient, efficient, and personalized services that meet the evolving needs of customers.

Harnessing the power of mobile technology and e-commerce is essential for businesses operating in the context of MSD. By embracing these technologies, businesses can enhance convenience, improve efficiency, and provide personalized experiences to customers, ultimately gaining a competitive advantage in the market.

Fostering Innovation and Entrepreneurship in Markets

Innovation and entrepreneurship are key drivers of economic growth and development in markets around the world. Fostering an environment that encourages and supports innovation and entrepreneurship is crucial for creating a thriving economy and ensuring long-term success. In this article, we will explore the importance of fostering innovation and entrepreneurship in markets, the benefits it brings, and the strategies that can be implemented to cultivate a culture of innovation and entrepreneurship.

Importance of Fostering Innovation and Entrepreneurship

Economic Growth: Innovation and entrepreneurship lead to the creation of new businesses, industries, and job opportunities, contributing to economic growth and prosperity.

Competitiveness: Markets that foster innovation and entrepreneurship are more competitive on a global scale. They attract investment, talent, and resources, which in turn drives innovation and the development of new products and services.

Problem Solving: Innovation and entrepreneurship are instrumental in addressing societal challenges and finding solutions to complex problems. They drive technological advancements, social progress, and sustainable development.

Job Creation: Entrepreneurs are known for creating new jobs and driving employment growth. By fostering innovation and entrepreneurship, markets can generate employment opportunities and reduce unemployment rates.

Resilience: Markets that embrace innovation and entrepreneurship are more resilient to economic downturns. By encouraging a diverse range of businesses and industries, they can adapt to changing market conditions and thrive in times of uncertainty.

Fostering innovation and entrepreneurship in markets is essential for economic growth, competitiveness, and societal progress. By implementing strategies that encourage education, access to funding, supportive regulations, collaboration, and recognition, markets can create an environment that nurtures innovation and empowers entrepreneurs to bring their ideas to life. This, in turn, leads to job creation, problem-solving, and a resilient economy that can thrive in today's dynamic and rapidly evolving world.

Chapter Four

Policy and Advocacy for Market Systems Development

Market Systems Development (MSD) is an approach that focuses on creating sustainable and inclusive market systems to drive economic growth and poverty reduction. While the implementation of MSD interventions is crucial, policy and advocacy play an equally important role in ensuring the long-term success and impact of these interventions. In this article, we will explore the significance of policy and advocacy in the context of MSD and discuss the strategies that can be employed to effectively promote and support market systems development.

Importance of Policy and Advocacy in MSD

Enabling Environment: Policy and advocacy efforts are essential for creating an enabling environment that supports market systems development. This involves developing favorable policies, regulations, and legal frameworks that encourage competition, protect property rights, and foster innovation.

Systemic Change: Policy and advocacy initiatives can drive systemic change by influencing government policies and regulations. By advocating for reforms that align with the principles of MSD, stakeholders can address systemic barriers and create an environment that promotes sustainable and inclusive market systems.

Collaboration and Coordination: Effective policy and advocacy require collaboration and coordination among various stakeholders, including government agencies, private sector actors, civil society organizations, and development partners. This collaboration ensures that the voices of different actors are heard and that policy interventions are well-informed and comprehensive.

Scaling Up and Replication: Policy and advocacy efforts can facilitate the scaling up and replication of successful market system development interventions. By promoting evidence-based practices and advocating for their adoption by government agencies and other stakeholders, the impact of MSD interventions can be expanded to reach a larger population.

Policy and advocacy play a pivotal role in supporting and advancing market systems development. By creating an enabling environment, driving systemic change, promoting collaboration, and advocating for evidence-based practices, stakeholders can ensure the sustainability and scalability of MSD interventions. With effective policy and advocacy efforts, market systems development can contribute significantly to economic growth, poverty reduction, and sustainable development.

Understanding Policy and Regulatory Frameworks

Policy and regulatory frameworks play a crucial role in Market Systems Development (MSD). These frameworks provide the necessary guidelines, rules, and incentives to create an enabling environment for sustainable and inclusive market systems. In this article, we will delve into the significance of policy and regulatory frameworks in MSD and explore how they can shape and support market systems development.

Components of Policy and Regulatory Frameworks in MSD

Legal and Regulatory Frameworks: These frameworks establish the legal basis for market operations and define the rights and responsibilities of market participants. They cover areas such as contract enforcement, property rights, competition policy, consumer protection, and environmental regulations.

Sector-Specific Policies: Sector-specific policies address the unique characteristics and challenges of different industries or sectors within the market system. They can include policies related to agriculture, finance, trade, infrastructure, and social protection, among others.

Institutional Arrangements: Policy and regulatory frameworks also encompass the institutional arrangements responsible for implementing and enforcing the rules and regulations. These institutions can include government agencies, regulatory bodies, industry associations, and civil society organizations.

Monitoring and Evaluation Mechanisms: Effective policy and regulatory frameworks require robust monitoring and evaluation mechanisms to assess their impact, identify gaps, and make necessary adjustments. These mechanisms ensure that policies are evidence-based, responsive, and adaptive to changing market dynamics.

Policy and Regulatory Challenges in MSD

Implementing effective policy and regulatory frameworks in MSD can be challenging due to various factors:

Lack of Capacity: Limited capacity within government agencies and other stakeholders can hinder the formulation, implementation, and enforcement of policies and regulations. Building the capacity of relevant institutions and individuals is crucial to overcome this challenge.

Coordination and Collaboration: Policy and regulatory frameworks often involve multiple stakeholders across different sectors. Ensuring effective coordination and collaboration among these stakeholders is essential for coherent and comprehensive policies.

Balancing Interests: Balancing the interests of various stakeholders, such as producers, consumers, and investors, is a complex task. Policymakers need to consider the diverse needs and priorities of these stakeholders while designing and implementing policies and regulations.

Policy Inertia: Shifting existing policies and regulations to align with market systems development principles can be challenging due to policy inertia. Overcoming resistance to change and fostering a culture of continuous policy improvement is crucial.

Policy and regulatory frameworks are fundamental to the success of Market Systems Development. They create an enabling environment, address market failures, promote inclusive growth, attract private sector investment, and facilitate innovation. By understanding and effectively shaping these frameworks, stakeholders can foster sustainable and inclusive market systems that drive economic growth and reduce poverty.

Role of Government in Market Systems

The government plays a pivotal role in Market Systems Development (MSD) by creating an enabling environment, promoting inclusive growth, and ensuring the stability and fairness of market systems. In this article, we will explore the various roles that governments can assume in supporting and guiding market systems development.

Creating an Enabling Environment: One of the primary roles of the government in MSD is to create an enabling environment for market systems to thrive. This involves establishing clear and transparent policies and regulations that foster competition, protect property rights, and ensure a level playing field for all market participants. Governments need to provide legal frameworks that support business operations, contract enforcement, and intellectual property rights. By creating a stable and predictable environment, governments can attract domestic and foreign investments, stimulate entrepreneurship, and facilitate economic growth.

Promoting Inclusive Growth: Governments also have a responsibility to promote inclusive growth within market systems. This involves ensuring that marginalized groups, such as women, youth, and small-scale farmers, have equal access to markets and opportunities. Governments can develop and implement policies that address structural inequalities and provide targeted support to these groups. They can support initiatives that enhance access to finance, strengthen value chains, and promote skills development and capacity building. By promoting inclusive growth, governments can reduce poverty and promote social and economic development.

Regulation and Oversight: Another crucial role of the government in market systems is regulation and oversight. Governments need to establish regulatory frameworks that protect consumers, ensure fair competition, and mitigate externalities. They need to monitor and enforce compliance with these regulations to maintain market integrity and prevent market failures. Governments can also play a role in monitoring and addressing issues related to market concentration, monopolistic practices, and anti-competitive behavior. By providing effective regulation and oversight, governments can safeguard the interests of market participants and maintain the stability and efficiency of market systems.

Facilitating Collaboration and Coordination: Governments also have a role to play in facilitating collaboration and coordination among various stakeholders in market systems. They can establish platforms for dialogue and engagement between the public and private sectors, civil society organizations, and academia. By fostering collaboration, governments can create opportunities for knowledge sharing, joint problem-solving, and the development of multi-stakeholder initiatives. Collaboration and coordination can lead to innovative solutions, improved policy formulation, and enhanced implementation of market systems development strategies.

The government's role in market systems development is multifaceted and vital. By creating an enabling environment, promoting inclusive growth, providing regulation and oversight, and facilitating collaboration and coordination, governments can support the development of sustainable and inclusive market systems. Governments need to strike a balance between providing support and guidance while allowing market forces to operate efficiently. With effective government intervention, market systems can drive economic growth, reduce poverty, and improve the well-being of individuals and communities.

Policy Formulation and Implementation Processes

Policy formulation and implementation processes are crucial components of Market Systems Development (MSD). Effective policies and their successful implementation are essential for creating an enabling environment, promoting inclusive growth, and ensuring the stability and sustainability of market systems. In this article, we will explore the importance of policy formulation and implementation in MSD.

Policy Formulation: Policy formulation in MSD involves the development and shaping of policies that support market systems development. This process typically starts with a comprehensive analysis of the market system, including identifying constraints and opportunities. Policy formulation requires close collaboration between government agencies, private sector actors, civil society organizations, and other stakeholders. It involves conducting research, gathering data, and engaging in consultations to ensure that policies are evidence-based, context-specific, and aligned with the needs and priorities of the market system.

During the policy formulation process, it is crucial to consider the potential impacts of policies on different actors within the market system. Policies should aim to promote inclusive growth, address inequalities, and ensure that marginalized groups have equal access to opportunities. Additionally, policies should be designed to encourage innovation, entrepreneurship, and sustainable development.

Policy Implementation: Policy implementation is the process of putting policies into practice. It involves translating policy objectives into concrete actions, programs, and initiatives. Successful implementation requires effective coordination, strong institutional frameworks, and adequate resources. Governments, in collaboration with relevant stakeholders, need to establish clear roles and responsibilities, monitor progress, and address any implementation challenges that may arise.

Policy implementation in MSD often involves multi-stakeholder engagement and collaboration. Governments need to work closely with private sector actors, civil society organizations, and development partners to ensure that policies are effectively implemented. Monitoring and evaluation mechanisms should be in place to assess the impact of policies and make necessary adjustments to improve their effectiveness.

Importance of Policy Formulation and Implementation in MSD:

Effective policy formulation and implementation are critical for the success of MSD. Well-designed policies can create an enabling environment that supports market systems development, attracts investments, and stimulates economic growth. Policies that promote inclusive growth help reduce poverty, create employment opportunities, and improve the livelihoods of individuals and communities. They can also contribute to sustainable development by addressing environmental challenges and promoting responsible business practices.

Policy formulation and implementation processes need to be participatory and transparent to ensure the legitimacy and ownership of policies. Consultations with relevant stakeholders and the engagement of marginalized groups are essential to ensure that policies are responsive to the needs and aspirations of all actors within the market system.

Policy formulation and implementation are vital elements of Market Systems Development. Effective policies that are well-formulated and successfully implemented can create an enabling environment for market systems to thrive, promote inclusive growth, and drive sustainable development. Governments, in collaboration with stakeholders, need to prioritize evidence-based policy formulation, ensure effective implementation, and continuously monitor and evaluate policies to achieve desired outcomes in MSD.

Creating Enabling Policy Environment for Market Development:

In the realm of Market Systems Development (MSD), creating an enabling policy environment is crucial for fostering sustainable market development and economic growth. Policies play a pivotal role in shaping market dynamics, promoting innovation, and ensuring fair competition. In this article, we will delve into the importance of creating an enabling policy environment for market development and explore key considerations in policy formulation and implementation.

Understanding an Enabling Policy Environment: An enabling policy environment refers to a set of policies and regulations that facilitate and support market development. It is characterized by policies that encourage entrepreneurship, attract investments, and remove barriers to market entry. Additionally, an enabling policy environment fosters fair competition, protects consumers, and promotes social and environmental responsibility.

The Role of Policy in Market Development: Policies have a profound impact on market dynamics and the overall business environment. They can either hinder or facilitate market development. Well-designed policies can create incentives for innovation, productivity, and investment, while poorly formulated or implemented policies can stifle market growth and hinder economic progress.

Key Considerations in Policy Formulation: Policy formulation in the context of market development requires a comprehensive understanding of the market system and its dynamics. It involves engaging with stakeholders, conducting in-depth research, and analyzing data to identify key challenges and opportunities. Policymakers should consider the specific needs and contexts of different market actors, including small and medium-sized enterprises (SMEs), marginalized groups, and vulnerable populations.

It is crucial for policies to be evidence-based and responsive to the evolving needs of the market. Policymakers should also prioritize stakeholder consultations to ensure that policies are inclusive and address the concerns of all relevant parties.

Implementation and Monitoring: The successful implementation of policies is equally important as their formulation. Effective coordination and collaboration between government agencies, private sector actors, and civil society organizations are essential for translating policies into actionable initiatives. Adequate resources, strong institutional frameworks, and monitoring mechanisms are necessary to track progress, evaluate impact, and make necessary adjustments.

Benefits of an Enabling Policy Environment: Creating an enabling policy environment has numerous benefits for market development. It attracts domestic and foreign investments, encourages entrepreneurship, and stimulates economic growth. A conducive policy environment promotes fair competition, leading to increased productivity and efficiency. It also enhances consumer protection, ensures social inclusivity, and supports sustainable development practices.

Creating an enabling policy environment is essential for market development. Well-formulated and effectively implemented policies can drive economic growth, foster innovation, and promote social and environmental responsibility. Policymakers should prioritize evidence-based policy formulation, stakeholder consultations, and continuous monitoring to ensure that policies align with market needs and contribute to sustainable and inclusive market development.

Advocacy is a powerful tool for MSD practitioners to drive positive change and promote sustainable market development. By employing research-based strategies, building alliances, engaging with policymakers, raising awareness, and utilizing effective communication, practitioners can effectively advocate for policy reforms and inclusive market practices. Through their advocacy efforts, MSD practitioners can contribute to creating an enabling environment that supports economic growth, innovation, and social inclusivity.

Building Alliances and Coalitions for Advocacy: Advocacy is a crucial component of Market Systems Development (MSD) that aims to drive positive change and promote sustainable market development. One effective strategy for successful advocacy in MSD is building alliances and coalitions. In this article, we will explore the importance of alliances and coalitions in advocacy efforts and discuss key strategies for building and leveraging these partnerships.

The Power of Alliances and Coalitions: Building alliances and coalitions is essential for effective advocacy in MSD. By joining forces with like-minded organizations, stakeholders, and networks, MSD practitioners can amplify their voices, share resources, and leverage collective expertise to advocate for policy reforms and inclusive market practices. These partnerships have the potential to create a stronger and more unified advocacy front, increasing the likelihood of success in driving systemic change.

Strategies for Building Alliances and Coalitions

Identify Shared Goals and Objectives: When building alliances and coalitions, it is crucial to identify organizations and stakeholders that share similar goals and objectives. This alignment ensures a common purpose and enhances collaboration towards advocating for specific changes within the market system.

Engage in Collaborative Planning: Effective alliances and coalitions require collaborative planning. MSD practitioners should work together with partner organizations to develop a shared advocacy strategy, including clear objectives, target audiences, messaging, and action plans. Collaborative planning allows for a coordinated and cohesive approach to advocacy efforts.

Establish Trust and Communication: Building alliances and coalitions is built on trust and effective communication. MSD practitioners should invest time and effort in establishing strong relationships with partner organizations, fostering open and transparent communication channels. Regular meetings, sharing of information, and joint decision-making processes help in building trust and maintaining effective collaboration.

Leverage Diverse Expertise: Alliances and coalitions bring together organizations with diverse expertise and perspectives. MSD practitioners should leverage this diversity by tapping into the unique strengths and capabilities of partner organizations. By combining technical knowledge, research capabilities, and grassroots connections, the coalition can develop comprehensive and evidence-based advocacy strategies.

Advocate for Mutual Interests: Successful alliances and coalitions are built on the principle of mutual benefit. MSD practitioners should ensure that the advocacy efforts align with the interests and priorities of partner organizations. By advocating for changes that benefit all stakeholders involved, the coalition can maintain solidarity and maximize its impact.

Engage in Joint Advocacy Activities: To effectively advocate for change, alliances and coalitions should engage in joint advocacy activities. This can include joint policy dialogues, joint research initiatives, joint campaigns, and joint representation at relevant forums. Joint advocacy activities demonstrate a unified front and amplify the impact of the advocacy message.

Building alliances and coalitions is a powerful strategy for effective advocacy in MSD. By identifying shared goals, engaging in collaborative planning, establishing trust and communication, leveraging diverse expertise, advocating for mutual interests, and engaging in joint advocacy activities, MSD practitioners can create a stronger and more impactful advocacy front. These partnerships enable practitioners to amplify their voices, share resources, and leverage collective expertise, ultimately driving positive change and promoting sustainable market development.

Engaging with Policy Makers and Influencers: Engaging with policy makers and influencers is a critical aspect of Market Systems Development (MSD) that can significantly impact the success of advocacy efforts. In this article, we will explore the importance of engaging with policy makers and influencers in MSD and discuss key strategies for effective engagement.

The Importance of Engaging with Policy Makers and Influencers: Policy makers and influencers play a pivotal role in shaping the economic and regulatory environment within which market systems operate. Engaging with these key stakeholders is crucial for driving policy reforms, promoting inclusive market practices, and creating an enabling environment for sustainable market development. By establishing strong relationships and effectively communicating with policy makers and influencers, MSD practitioners can advocate for positive change and influence policy decisions.

Strategies for Effective Engagement

Build Relationships: Building relationships with policy makers and influencers is the foundation for effective engagement. MSD practitioners should invest time and effort in understanding their interests, priorities, and decision-making processes. Developing personal connections and maintaining regular communication can help establish trust and credibility, making it easier to influence policy decisions.

Demonstrate the Value of MSD: MSD practitioners should effectively communicate the value and impact of their work to policy makers and influencers. Providing evidence-based research, case studies, and success stories can help them understand the positive outcomes that can be achieved through MSD. Demonstrating the potential for job creation, poverty reduction, and economic growth can make a compelling case for policy reforms.

Tailor Messages to the Audience: When engaging with policy makers and influencers, it is important to tailor messages to their specific needs and interests. MSD practitioners should craft messages that resonate with their priorities and demonstrate how MSD aligns with their broader policy objectives. Highlighting the potential for collaboration and mutual benefits can generate interest and support for MSD initiatives.

Collaborate in Policy Development: Engaging with policy makers and influencers during the policy development process is crucial. MSD practitioners should actively participate in policy dialogues, consultations, and working groups to ensure that the voices of the market system actors are represented. By providing technical expertise, evidence-based recommendations, and practical insights, they can contribute to the development of policies that promote inclusive market practices.

Leverage Influencers and Networks: Influencers and networks can have a significant impact on policy makers' decisions. MSD practitioners should identify and engage with influential individuals and organizations who can advocate for MSD initiatives. Leveraging their expertise, credibility, and networks can help amplify the advocacy message and increase the likelihood of policy reforms.

Continuously Monitor and Evaluate: Engaging with policy makers and influencers is an ongoing process. MSD practitioners should continuously monitor policy developments, evaluate the effectiveness of engagement strategies, and adapt their approach accordingly. Regular evaluation allows for course correction, identification of new opportunities, and continuous improvement in advocacy efforts.

Engaging with policy makers and influencers is crucial for driving policy reforms and promoting inclusive market practices in MSD. By building relationships, demonstrating the value of MSD, tailoring messages, collaborating in policy development, leveraging influencers and networks, and continuously monitoring and evaluating engagement strategies, MSD practitioners can effectively advocate for positive change and influence policy decisions. Successful engagement with policy makers and influencers can create an enabling environment for sustainable market development, leading to economic growth, poverty reduction, and improved livelihoods.

Communicating the Benefits of MSD to Stakeholders

When implementing a new system or technology, it's crucial to effectively communicate the benefits to stakeholders. This ensures that everyone involved understands the value and potential impact of the system. In the case of Market Systems Development (MSD), which aims to improve efficiency and productivity in all processes, clear communication is essential. In this article, we will explore the importance of communicating the benefits of MSD to stakeholders and provide strategies for effective communication.

Importance of Communicating MSD Benefits

Alignment of Expectations: One of the main reasons for communicating the benefits of MSD to stakeholders is to align expectations. Stakeholders, such as management, employees, and investors, need to understand how the system will improve operations and contribute to the overall success of the organization. By clearly communicating the benefits, you can ensure that everyone shares a common vision and has realistic expectations.

Support and Buy-In: Effective communication of the benefits of MSD can help generate support and buy-in from stakeholders. When stakeholders understand how the system will positively impact the organization, they are more likely to support its implementation and actively participate in the process. This support is crucial for the successful adoption and implementation of the MSD system.

Overcoming Resistance to Change: Implementing a new system like MSD often faces resistance from stakeholders who are comfortable with the existing processes. By communicating the benefits of the system, you can address concerns, dispel misconceptions, and help stakeholders understand the need for change. This can help overcome resistance and create a more positive and receptive environment for the adoption of MSD.

Monitoring and Evaluation of MSD Programs

Monitoring and evaluation (M&E) are crucial components of any Market Systems Development (MSD) program. M&E ensures that the program is on track, objectives are being met, and necessary adjustments can be made for optimal results. In this article, we will explore the importance of monitoring and evaluation in MSD programs and discuss key aspects of effective M&E.

Importance of Monitoring and Evaluation

Tracking Progress: Monitoring and evaluation allow stakeholders to track the progress of the MSD program. By regularly monitoring key indicators and evaluating the outcomes, stakeholders can identify if the program is meeting its objectives, optimize processes, and make informed decisions based on data. This helps ensure that the program remains aligned with the organization's goals and delivers the intended benefits.

Identifying Challenges and Opportunities: M&E provides valuable insights into the challenges and opportunities encountered during the implementation of the MSD program. It helps identify bottlenecks, areas for improvement, and potential risks that may hinder the program's success. By identifying these issues early on, stakeholders can take proactive measures to address them, optimize operations, and capitalize on opportunities for further improvement.

Accountability and Learning: Monitoring and evaluation promote accountability within the MSD program. It allows stakeholders to assess the effectiveness of their strategies and actions, holding them accountable for their performance. Additionally, M&E enables organizations to learn from their experiences, both successes, and failures, and apply these lessons to future initiatives. This iterative learning process helps drive continuous improvement and innovation within the organization.

Key Aspects of Effective M&E in MSD Programs

Clear Objectives and Indicators: To effectively monitor and evaluate an MSD program, clear objectives and indicators must be established. Objectives should be specific, measurable, achievable, relevant, and time-bound (SMART). Indicators should be selected to track progress towards the objectives and provide meaningful data for evaluation. By defining objectives and indicators at the outset, stakeholders can ensure that the M&E process is focused and aligned with the desired outcomes.

Data Collection and Analysis: Collecting and analyzing relevant data is essential for effective M&E. Stakeholders should identify the key data points and sources required to assess the progress and impact of the MSD program. This may include data on productivity, quality, cost savings, employee satisfaction, and customer feedback. Data should be collected consistently, accurately, and on a regular basis. Analysis of the data should be done systematically, using appropriate statistical methods and tools, to derive meaningful insights and inform decision-making.

Continuous Feedback and Adaptation: M&E should be an ongoing process that includes continuous feedback and adaptation. Regular feedback loops should be established to gather input from stakeholders, including employees, managers, and customers. This feedback can help identify emerging issues, validate assumptions, and inform necessary adjustments to the program. By staying responsive and adaptable, stakeholders can ensure that the MSD program remains relevant and effective in a dynamic Market environment.

Monitoring and evaluation are vital for the success of MSD programs. They provide stakeholders with the means to track progress, identify challenges and opportunities, promote accountability, and drive continuous improvement. By establishing clear objectives and indicators, collecting and analyzing relevant data, and fostering a culture of continuous feedback and adaptation, stakeholders can ensure that their MSD programs deliver optimal results and contribute to the overall success of the organization.

Developing Monitoring and Evaluation Frameworks

Developing a robust monitoring and evaluation (M&E) framework is crucial for effective implementation and success of Market Systems Development (MSD) programs. M&E frameworks provide a structured approach to systematically track progress, measure impact, and make data-driven decisions. In this article, we will explore the importance of developing M&E frameworks in the context of MSD and discuss key considerations for their development.

Importance of Developing M&E Frameworks

Clear Objectives and Target: Developing an M&E framework helps clarify the objectives and targets of the MSD program. It provides a roadmap for measuring progress towards these objectives and ensures alignment with the organization's overall goals. By establishing clear objectives and targets, stakeholders can effectively assess the impact of the program and identify areas for improvement.

Accountability and Learning: An M&E framework promotes accountability within the MSD program. It sets up mechanisms to measure and evaluate performance, hold stakeholders accountable for their actions, and learn from the outcomes. Through regular monitoring and evaluation, stakeholders can identify successes, challenges, and lessons learned, allowing for continuous improvement and innovation.

Evidence-Based Decision-Making: An M&E framework enables evidence-based decision-making in the MSD program. By collecting and analyzing relevant data, stakeholders can make informed decisions, identify areas of improvement, and optimize resource allocation. This data-driven approach ensures that decisions are based on objective evidence, leading to more effective and efficient program implementation.

Key Considerations for Developing M&E Frameworks in MSD

Clearly Defined Indicators: Developing an M&E framework requires clearly defined indicators that align with the objectives of the MSD program. Indicators should be specific, measurable, attainable, relevant, and time-bound (SMART). They should capture both quantitative and qualitative aspects of the program's impact, such as productivity gains, cost savings, quality improvements, and employee satisfaction. By selecting appropriate indicators, stakeholders can effectively track progress and measure the success of the program.

Data Collection and Analysis: An effective M&E framework includes mechanisms for systematic data collection and analysis. Stakeholders should identify the data sources, collection methods, and tools required to gather relevant data. This may include surveys, interviews, observations, and existing data sources such as production records and employee feedback. Data should be collected consistently and accurately and analyzed using appropriate methods and tools to derive meaningful insights.

Regular Monitoring and Evaluation: Developing an M&E framework involves establishing a regular monitoring and evaluation cycle. This ensures that progress is tracked at various intervals throughout the program's implementation. Regular monitoring allows stakeholders to identify issues, make timely adjustments, and assess the effectiveness of interventions. Evaluation, on the other hand, provides a comprehensive assessment of the program's impact and helps inform future decision-making.

Developing a comprehensive monitoring and evaluation framework is essential for the success of MSD programs. It provides stakeholders with a structured approach to measure progress, promote accountability, and make evidence-based decisions. By establishing clear objectives and targets, defining relevant indicators, collecting and analyzing data, and implementing regular monitoring and evaluation cycles, stakeholders can ensure that their MSD programs contribute to the overall success of the organization.

Indicators and Measurement of Market System Change

Indicators and measurement are critical components of monitoring and evaluating Market System Development (MSD) programs. In the context of MSD, indicators serve as measurable parameters that provide insights into the changes occurring within market systems. These indicators help stakeholders understand the impact of interventions, track progress, and make informed decisions. In this article, we will explore the importance of indicators and measurement in MSD and discuss key considerations for their implementation.

Importance of Indicators and Measurement

Tracking Change in Market Systems: Indicators provide a means to track changes within market systems. They help stakeholders measure progress towards desired outcomes, identify bottlenecks and barriers, and assess the effectiveness of interventions. By monitoring indicators over time, stakeholders can gain insights into the dynamic nature of market systems and make data-driven decisions to drive positive change.

Assessing Impact and Effectiveness: Indicators and measurement techniques enable stakeholders to assess the impact and effectiveness of interventions in MSD programs. By comparing baseline and endline data, stakeholders can determine the extent to which interventions have influenced market systems. This assessment helps identify successful interventions, areas for improvement, and lessons learned for future program design and implementation.

Accountability and Learning: Indicators and measurement contribute to accountability and learning within MSD programs. They provide a framework for stakeholders to track their own performance, evaluate the effectiveness of their strategies, and learn from successes and failures. By holding themselves accountable and continuously learning, stakeholders can adapt their approaches and drive sustainable change within market systems.

Key Considerations for Indicators and Measurement in MSD

Relevance and Alignment: Indicators should be relevant to the specific context and goals of the MSD program. They should align with the desired outcomes and capture the changes that are most meaningful to the market system. Stakeholders should carefully select indicators that reflect the specific challenges, opportunities, and dynamics of the target market, ensuring that they provide a comprehensive understanding of the changes occurring within the system.

Data Collection and Analysis: Collecting and analyzing data is a crucial aspect of implementing indicators in MSD programs. Stakeholders must determine the appropriate data collection methods, tools, and sources to capture the relevant information. This may involve surveys, interviews, focus group discussions, secondary data analysis, and other data collection techniques. It is important to ensure the accuracy, reliability, and consistency of data collection processes to generate reliable insights.

Participatory Approach: Indicators and measurement should involve a participatory approach, engaging key stakeholders throughout the process. Collaborative engagement with market actors, local communities, and other relevant parties can provide valuable insights and ensure that indicators reflect the diverse perspectives and needs of the market system. This participatory approach fosters ownership, enhances data quality, and increases the relevance and effectiveness of the indicators.

Indicators and measurement are essential components of MSD programs as they enable stakeholders to track progress, assess impact, and promote accountability and learning. By selecting relevant indicators, implementing robust data collection and analysis processes, and adopting a participatory approach, stakeholders can effectively measure and understand the changes occurring within market systems. With this knowledge, they can make informed decisions, adapt strategies, and drive sustainable change for the betterment of the market system and its participants.

Learning and Adaptation in MSD Interventions

In Market System Development (MSD), learning and adaptation are crucial elements of successful interventions. MSD programs aim to bring about systemic change within market systems, and learning from the implementation process is essential for effective adaptation and continuous improvement. In this article, we will explore the importance of learning and adaptation in MSD interventions and discuss key considerations for incorporating these elements into program design and implementation.

Importance of Learning and Adaptation

Flexibility and Responsiveness: Learning and adaptation allow MSD interventions to be flexible and responsive to the dynamic nature of market systems. By continuously gathering feedback, analyzing data, and monitoring progress, stakeholders can identify emerging trends, challenges, and opportunities. This enables them to make informed decisions and adapt their strategies accordingly, ensuring that interventions remain relevant and effective.

Maximizing Impact: Learning from MSD interventions helps stakeholders maximize their impact within market systems. By analyzing data and evaluating the outcomes of interventions, stakeholders can identify successful approaches, scale up effective strategies, and modify or discontinue interventions that are not generating the desired results. This iterative process of learning and adaptation increases the likelihood of achieving sustainable and transformative change.

Collaboration and Knowledge Sharing: Learning and adaptation foster collaboration and knowledge sharing among stakeholders involved in MSD interventions. By sharing lessons learned, best practices, and innovative ideas, stakeholders can collectively address challenges, build on each other's successes, and avoid duplicating efforts. This collaborative approach enhances the effectiveness and efficiency of interventions, leading to more impactful outcomes.

Key Considerations for Learning and Adaptation in MSD Interventions

Monitoring and Evaluation: Monitoring and evaluation (M&E) play a critical role in facilitating learning and adaptation in MSD interventions. Robust M&E systems enable stakeholders to collect and analyze relevant data, track progress towards desired outcomes, and assess the impact of interventions. It is important to establish clear indicators, data collection methods, and evaluation frameworks from the outset to ensure that learning can take place effectively.

Participatory Approach: A participatory approach is essential for learning and adaptation in MSD interventions. Engaging market actors, local communities, and other stakeholders throughout the process fosters ownership, encourages diverse perspectives, and ensures that interventions align with the needs and aspirations of the market system. This participatory approach enhances the relevance and effectiveness of interventions and promotes sustainable change.

Knowledge Management and Learning Platforms: Establishing knowledge management systems and learning platforms is crucial for capturing and disseminating lessons learned from MSD interventions. These platforms can include databases, case studies, communities of practice, and learning events. By documenting and sharing knowledge, stakeholders can facilitate cross-learning, encourage innovation, and build a collective understanding of what works and what doesn't in MSD interventions.

Learning and adaptation are essential for successful MSD interventions. By embracing a flexible and responsive approach, stakeholders can maximize their impact, foster collaboration, and drive sustainable change within market systems. Through robust monitoring and evaluation, a participatory approach, and effective knowledge management, stakeholders can continuously learn, adapt, and improve their interventions, ultimately leading to transformative change and positive outcomes for the market system and its participants.

Chapter Five

Case Studies in Market System Development

Case studies play a crucial role in Market System Development (MSD) as they provide valuable insights into the challenges, successes, and lessons learned from implementing interventions within market systems. These real-world examples offer practitioners and stakeholders a deeper understanding of the complexities of MSD and inform future program design and implementation. In this article, we will explore the significance of case studies in MSD and discuss how they contribute to learning, adaptation, and evidence-based decision making.

Successful MSD Interventions in Agriculture Sector

Market System Development (MSD) interventions in the agriculture sector have proven to be effective in addressing challenges and improving the livelihoods of smallholder farmers. These interventions focus on transforming market systems to create sustainable and inclusive agricultural value chains. In this article, we will explore successful MSD interventions in the agriculture sector, highlighting their impact, key strategies, and lessons learned.

Impact of MSD Interventions in Agriculture

Increased Productivity and Income: Successful MSD interventions in the agriculture sector have led to increased productivity and income for smallholder farmers. By providing access to improved technologies, inputs, and market linkages, these interventions have helped farmers enhance their production practices and connect with higher-value markets. This has resulted in improved yields, increased sales, and higher incomes for farmers.

Strengthened Market Linkages: MSD interventions have played a vital role in strengthening market linkages within the agriculture sector. By facilitating connections between farmers, input suppliers, processors, and buyers, these interventions have created more efficient and transparent value chains. This has led to better market access, reduced transaction costs, and improved bargaining power for smallholder farmers.

Improved Resilience and Adaptability: Successful MSD interventions have also focused on building the resilience and adaptability of smallholder farmers. By promoting climate-smart agricultural practices, diversification of income sources, and access to financial services, these interventions have helped farmers mitigate risks and cope with shocks. This has enhanced their ability to withstand challenges such as climate change, market fluctuations, and economic uncertainties.

Improving Agricultural Value Chain

Agricultural value chains play a crucial role in the global food system, connecting farmers to consumers and facilitating the movement of agricultural products. However, these value chains often face various challenges such as inefficiencies, lack of market access, and limited opportunities for smallholder farmers. Market System Development (MSD) approaches have emerged as effective strategies to improve agricultural value chains, creating more inclusive and sustainable systems. In this article, we will explore the importance of improving agricultural value chains through MSD interventions, key strategies, and the potential benefits for both farmers and consumers.

Potential Benefits of Improved Agricultural Value Chains

Increased Incomes for Farmers: By improving market access, reducing transaction costs, and enhancing productivity, MSD interventions in agricultural value chains can lead to increased incomes for farmers. This provides them with the financial stability to invest in their farms, adopt modern technologies, and improve their overall standard of living.

Enhanced Food Security and Nutrition: Improvements in agricultural value chains can contribute to enhanced food security and nutrition. By strengthening supply chains, reducing post-harvest losses, and ensuring the availability of nutritious food, MSD interventions improve access to safe and healthy food for consumers. This, in turn, leads to improved nutrition outcomes, particularly in vulnerable communities.

Sustainable Agricultural Practices: MSD interventions promote sustainable agricultural practices by encouraging the adoption of climate-smart techniques, resource-efficient farming methods, and environmentally friendly production and processing practices. This contributes to the preservation of natural resources, reduces the environmental footprint of agriculture, and supports the transition towards a more sustainable food system.

Improving agricultural value chains through MSD interventions is crucial for creating inclusive, efficient, and sustainable food systems. By addressing market failures, strengthening market linkages, and empowering smallholder farmers, these interventions have the potential to enhance productivity, increase incomes, and improve food security and nutrition. Key strategies, such as stakeholder collaboration, capacity building, and market research, contribute to the success of these interventions. Ultimately, by investing in the improvement of agricultural value chains, we can create a more resilient and equitable food system that benefits both farmers and consumers alike.

Enhancing Access to Inputs and Finance: Access to inputs and finance is crucial for farmers and agricultural businesses to thrive and improve productivity. However, many smallholder farmers and entrepreneurs face significant barriers in accessing these essential resources. Market System Development (MSD) approaches offer effective strategies to enhance access to inputs and finance, enabling farmers to optimize their operations and unlock their full potential. In this article, we will explore the importance of enhancing access to inputs and finance through MSD interventions, key strategies employed, and the potential benefits for farmers and the agricultural sector.

Strengthening Farmer Organizations and Cooperatives

Farmer organizations and cooperatives play a pivotal role in the agricultural sector by empowering smallholder farmers, promoting collective action, and facilitating market access. However, many of these organizations face challenges such as limited capacity, weak governance structures, and inadequate market linkages. Market System Development (MSD) approaches offer effective strategies to strengthen farmer organizations and cooperatives, enabling them to become resilient, sustainable, and influential actors in the agricultural value chain. In this article, we will explore the importance of strengthening farmer organizations and cooperatives through MSD interventions, key strategies employed, and the potential benefits for farmers and the broader agricultural sector.

Importance of Strengthening Farmer Organizations and Cooperatives

Enhancing Farmer Voice and Representation: Farmer organizations and cooperatives provide a platform for collective action and amplify the voice of smallholder farmers. By strengthening these organizations, MSD interventions empower farmers to advocate for their interests, engage in policy dialogues, and influence decision-making processes at local, regional, and national levels.

Building Market Power and Negotiating Strength: Collective action through farmer organizations and cooperatives allows smallholder farmers to pool their resources, aggregate their produce, and negotiate better prices and market terms with buyers and input suppliers. By providing a unified front, these organizations enable farmers to overcome market barriers, access higher-value markets, and capture a larger share of the value chain.

Facilitating Knowledge Sharing and Capacity Building: Farmer organizations and cooperatives serve as platforms for knowledge-sharing, capacity building, and peer learning. Through training programs and technical assistance, MSD interventions empower farmers with the necessary skills and knowledge to improve their farming practices, adopt sustainable techniques, and implement innovative approaches. This fosters continuous learning and professional development within the farming community.

Key Strategies in Strengthening Farmer Organizations and Cooperatives

Institutional Strengthening and Governance: MSD interventions focus on strengthening the institutional capacity and governance structures of farmer organizations and cooperatives. This involves providing training on leadership, financial management, and organizational development, as well as supporting the establishment of transparent and accountable governance systems. By enhancing their internal operations, these organizations become more efficient, resilient, and better equipped to serve their members' needs.

Market Linkages and Access to Services: MSD approaches facilitate market linkages between farmer organizations and key actors in the value chain, such as buyers, processors, and input suppliers. By creating direct connections and partnerships, these interventions enable farmers to access essential services, including credit, inputs, machinery, and technical assistance. This enhances their productivity, reduces production costs, and improves their overall competitiveness in the market.

Advocacy and Networking: MSD interventions support farmer organizations and cooperatives in advocacy efforts, enabling them to influence policies, regulations, and market practices. By fostering networking opportunities and facilitating collaboration among different stakeholders, these interventions strengthen the collective voice of farmers and promote inclusive and sustainable agricultural development.

MSD Approaches in Micro, Small, and Medium Enterprises (MSMEs)

Micro, Small, and Medium Enterprises (MSMEs) play a crucial role in economic development, job creation, and poverty alleviation. However, these enterprises often face significant challenges in terms of access to markets, finance, technology, and skills. Market Systems Development (MSD) approaches have emerged as effective strategies to address these challenges and promote sustainable growth and development in MSMEs. In this article, we will explore the key MSD approaches and their impact on MSMEs.

MSD approaches have demonstrated their effectiveness in promoting inclusive and sustainable growth in MSMEs. By addressing market constraints and empowering MSMEs, these approaches contribute to poverty reduction, job creation, and economic development. However, it is essential to tailor MSD interventions to the specific context and needs of MSMEs to ensure their long-term success and impact.

Promoting MSMEs in Urban and Rural Areas

Micro, Small, and Medium Enterprises (MSMEs) are vital drivers of economic growth and development in both urban and rural areas. However, there are distinct challenges and opportunities when it comes to promoting and supporting MSMEs in these different contexts. In this article, we will explore the strategies and approaches for promoting MSMEs in both urban and rural areas.

Urban Areas: In urban areas, MSMEs benefit from a dense population, access to markets, infrastructure, and a skilled labor force. To promote MSMEs in urban areas, the following strategies can be implemented:

1) **Access to Markets**: Urban MSMEs can take advantage of the proximity to a large customer base and establish strong connections with wholesalers, retailers, and distributors. Developing market linkages, participating in trade fairs and exhibitions, and leveraging e-commerce platforms can help urban MSMEs expand their market reach.
2) **Technology Adoption**: Urban MSMEs can benefit from adopting innovative technologies and digital solutions to enhance productivity, streamline operations, and reach new customers. Embracing e-commerce, digital marketing, and online payment systems can give urban MSMEs a competitive edge.
3) **Networking and Collaboration**: Urban MSMEs can leverage the advantages of networking and collaboration to access resources, share knowledge, and collectively address common challenges. Participating in business associations, industry clusters, and entrepreneurship networks can facilitate collaboration among urban MSMEs.
4) **Rural Areas**: Rural areas present unique challenges such as limited infrastructure, access to markets, and a skilled labor force. However, there are specific strategies that can be employed to promote MSMEs in rural areas:
5) **Value Chain Development**: By focusing on value chain development, rural MSMEs can enhance their competitiveness and access higher-value markets. This

involves strengthening the linkages between producers, processors, and distributors, improving product quality, and adopting sustainable production practices.

6) **Access to Finance**: Access to finance is critical for rural MSMEs to invest in their businesses and expand operations. Promoting microfinance institutions, establishing rural banking facilities, and providing financial literacy programs can improve access to finance for rural MSMEs.

7) **Skill Development and Training**: Developing the skills and capabilities of rural MSME owners and workers is crucial for their growth and success. Providing training programs, vocational education, and technical assistance can enhance their productivity and enable them to adapt to changing market dynamics.

8) **Government Support**: Governments can play a pivotal role in promoting rural MSMEs by providing incentives, subsidies, and infrastructure development. Policies that facilitate business registration, simplify licensing procedures, and offer tax incentives can attract investment and stimulate rural MSME growth.

It is important to recognize that promoting MSMEs in both urban and rural areas requires tailored and context-specific approaches. By addressing the unique challenges and leveraging the opportunities in each setting, MSMEs can thrive and contribute to inclusive and sustainable economic development.

Supporting business development services for MSMEs is essential for their growth, competitiveness, and long-term sustainability. By addressing the specific needs and challenges of MSMEs and providing them with access to finance, capacity building, market linkages, technology adoption, and policy support, these services can empower MSMEs to thrive and contribute to economic development. It is crucial for governments, non-profit organizations, and other stakeholders to prioritize and invest in these services to unlock the full potential of MSMEs.

Facilitating market linkages for MSMEs is essential for their growth, expansion, and ability to compete in the global marketplace. By providing market research, networking opportunities, access to market information, e-commerce support, and capacity building programs, business development services can empower MSMEs to establish valuable business relationships, access new markets, and achieve sustainable growth. It is imperative for governments, industry associations, and other stakeholders to invest in and prioritize these strategies to unlock the full potential of MSMEs and foster economic development.

Market System Development in Conflict-Affected Areas

Market system development plays a crucial role in post-conflict reconstruction and economic recovery in conflict-affected areas. In these regions, the impact of conflict on local markets is significant, with disrupted supply chains, damaged infrastructure, and a weakened business environment. Facilitating market system development is essential to rebuild livelihoods, create employment opportunities, and foster economic stability. In this article, we will explore the importance of market system development in conflict-affected areas and the key strategies that can be employed to achieve sustainable economic growth.

Market system development in conflict-affected areas is vital for post-conflict reconstruction, economic recovery, and stability. By assessing market systems, strengthening market institutions, rehabilitating infrastructure, improving access to finance, and providing skills development and training, development practitioners can create an enabling environment for market actors to thrive. It is crucial for international organizations, governments, and local stakeholders to collaborate and invest in sustainable market system development strategies to promote economic growth, reduce poverty, and build resilient communities in conflict-affected areas.

Addressing Market Disruptions and Fragilities

Market disruptions and fragilities can have severe consequences on economies and livelihoods, particularly in times of crises or shocks. These disruptions can arise from various factors, such as natural disasters, economic downturns, political instability, or health emergencies. It is essential to address these market challenges promptly and effectively to mitigate their impact and foster economic resilience. In this article, we will explore strategies for addressing market disruptions and fragilities, ensuring stability and promoting sustainable economic growth.

Addressing market disruptions and fragilities is crucial for maintaining economic stability, protecting livelihoods, and fostering sustainable growth. By strengthening market monitoring and analysis, ensuring supply chain resilience, promoting market diversification, facilitating access to finance and credit, and strengthening social safety nets, policymakers and development practitioners can effectively respond to market challenges and create a more resilient and inclusive economy. It is essential for governments, international organizations, and stakeholders to work together to implement these strategies and build economies that are better prepared to withstand and recover from market disruptions.

Building Resilience and Economic Recovery

Building resilience and promoting economic recovery are critical in times of crisis or economic downturns. Whether it's a natural disaster, a global pandemic, or a financial crisis, the ability to bounce back and ensure long-term stability is essential for individuals, businesses, and economies as a whole. In this article, we will explore strategies for building resilience and fostering economic recovery to navigate through challenging times.

Building resilience and promoting economic recovery are essential for navigating through challenging times and fostering long-term stability. By strengthening infrastructure, promoting diversification, fostering innovation and technology adoption, enhancing access to finance, investing in human capital, and strengthening social safety nets, economies can bounce back from crises, create sustainable growth, and ensure the well-being of their citizens. It requires collaboration between governments, businesses, and stakeholders to implement these strategies effectively and build resilient economies.

Promoting Peacebuilding through Market Development

Promoting peacebuilding is crucial for societies recovering from conflict and striving for long-term stability. While traditional approaches to peacebuilding often focus on political negotiations and security measures, market development can play a significant role in fostering peace and reconciliation. In this article, we will explore the connection between market development and peacebuilding and how economic growth can contribute to sustainable peace.

Economic Opportunities: One of the key drivers of conflict is the lack of economic opportunities. High unemployment rates and limited access to income-generating activities can create frustration and resentment, leading to social unrest and violence. By promotgrowth and development, governments and international organizations can create jobs, stimulate economic growth, and provide individuals with a sense of purpose and stability. Economic opportunities not only address the root causes of conflict but also contribute to social cohesion and stability.

Trade and Interdependence: Market development promotes trade and economic interdependence between communities and countries. Increased trade fosters cooperation, reduces tensions, and builds mutual trust among different groups. By facilitating economic exchanges and encouraging collaboration, market development can bridge divides and promote peaceful coexistence. Moreover, trade can help break down barriers and prejudices, fostering a sense of shared prosperity and reducing the likelihood of conflict.

Reintegration and Reconciliation: Market development initiatives can facilitate the reintegration of former combatants into society and promote reconciliation. By providing vocational training, access to credit, and entrepreneurship support, ex-combatants can reintegrate into the economy and contribute to their communities' development. Economic opportunities enable individuals to rebuild their lives and establish relationships based on trust and cooperation, thereby fostering reconciliation and healing.

Infrastructure Development: Market development often involves investing in infrastructure, such as transportation networks, energy systems, and telecommunications. Improved infrastructure not only facilitates economic activities but also enhances connectivity and access to basic services. By providing communities with reliable infrastructure, market development can promote inclusivity and reduce disparities, addressing grievances and promoting peace.

Social and Economic Inclusion: Market development initiatives should prioritize social and economic inclusion, ensuring that marginalized groups, such as women, youth, and minority communities, have equal access to economic opportunities. By promoting gender equality, empowering marginalized groups, and addressing social inequalities, market development can promote social cohesion and reduce the risk of conflict.

Promoting peacebuilding through market development is a holistic and sustainable approach to achieving long-lasting peace and stability. By creating economic opportunities, fostering trade and interdependence, facilitating reintegration and reconciliation, investing in infrastructure, and promoting social and economic inclusion, market development can contribute to sustainable peace. It requires collaborative efforts between governments, international organizations, and local communities to implement market-driven initiatives that address the root causes of conflict and promote inclusive economic growth. Through market development, societies can rebuild, reconcile, and thrive, paving the way for a peaceful and prosperous future.

Chapter Six

Partnerships and Collaboration

In the field of Market Systems Development (MSD), partnerships and collaboration are vital for achieving sustainable and inclusive economic growth. MSD is an approach that focuses on strengthening market systems to improve the livelihoods of individuals and communities. By fostering partnerships and collaboration among different stakeholders, MSD initiatives can maximize their impact and create lasting change. In this article, we will explore the importance of partnerships and collaboration in MSD and the benefits they bring.

Partnerships and collaboration are fundamental to effective Market Systems Development. By embracing a multi-stakeholder approach, coordinating efforts, leveraging expertise and resources, fostering innovation and learning, and achieving sustainability and scale, MSD initiatives can drive inclusive economic growth and improve the livelihoods of individuals and communities. Through collaborative efforts, stakeholders can create lasting impact and contribute to the development of vibrant and resilient market systems.

Engaging with Private Sector in MSD Initiatives

Engaging with the private sector is crucial in the success of Market Systems Development (MSD) initiatives. The private sector plays a vital role in driving economic growth, creating jobs, and fostering innovation. By collaborating with private sector actors, MSD initiatives can harness their expertise, resources, and market knowledge to bring about sustainable and inclusive development. In this article, we will explore the importance of engaging with the private sector in MSD initiatives and the benefits it brings.

Engaging with Private Sector in MSD Initiatives

Engaging with the private sector is a crucial component of Market Systems Development (MSD) initiatives. The private sector plays a vital role in driving economic growth, creating jobs, and fostering innovation. By partnering with private sector actors, MSD initiatives can leverage their resources, expertise, and market knowledge to achieve sustainable and inclusive development. In this article, we will explore the importance of engaging with the private sector in MSD initiatives and discuss the benefits and challenges associated with such collaborations.

Engaging with the private sector is essential for the success of MSD initiatives. By partnering with private sector actors, MSD initiatives can access resources, expertise, and market knowledge, adopt market-based approaches, drive job creation and economic growth, foster collaboration and partnerships, and achieve sustainable and inclusive development. However, it is important to address challenges and considerations associated with private sector engagement to ensure that the benefits are shared equitably and responsible business practices are upheld. Through effective collaboration between the public and private sectors, MSD initiatives can create lasting impact and contribute to the achievement of sustainable development goals.

Corporate Social Responsibility and Shared Value Approaches

Corporate Social Responsibility (CSR) and Shared Value approaches are two distinct but related concepts that aim to integrate social and environmental considerations into business strategies. Both approaches recognize the importance of businesses taking responsibility for their impact on society and the environment. In this article, we will explore the key principles and benefits of CSR and Shared Value approaches.

Corporate Social Responsibility (CSR): CSR refers to a company's voluntary actions to address social, environmental, and ethical issues beyond legal requirements. It involves integrating responsible business practices into core operations and engaging with stakeholders to create positive social and environmental impact. CSR initiatives can include philanthropy, employee volunteering, environmental sustainability efforts, and ethical sourcing practices. The overarching goal of CSR is to contribute to sustainable development and improve the well-being of communities and the planet.

Shared Value: Shared Value is a concept introduced by Michael Porter and Mark Kramer that goes beyond traditional CSR. It focuses on creating economic value while simultaneously addressing societal challenges.

Shared Value approaches seek to align business interests with social needs, recognizing that business success and social progress are interrelated. By identifying and addressing social issues through their core business activities, companies can create shared value for both them and society. This can be achieved through innovation, inclusive business models, supply chain improvements, and community partnerships.

Benefits of CSR and Shared Value approaches:

Enhanced Reputation: Engaging in CSR and Shared Value initiatives can improve a company's reputation and brand image. Stakeholders, including customers, employees, and investors, are increasingly interested in supporting socially responsible businesses.

Increased Employee Engagement: CSR and Shared Value initiatives can boost employee morale and engagement. Employees are often more motivated to work for companies that have a positive impact on society and the environment.

Improved Risk Management: Integrating social and environmental considerations into business strategies can help mitigate risks associated with regulatory compliance, reputational damage, and supply chain disruptions.

Access to New Markets: CSR and Shared Value approaches can open opportunities in new markets by addressing social needs and meeting the demands of socially conscious consumers.

Long-term Sustainability: By integrating responsible practices into their operations, companies can contribute to long-term sustainability and the achievement of the UN Sustainable Development Goals.

Both CSR and Shared Value approaches are valuable frameworks for businesses to contribute positively to society and the environment. While CSR focuses on voluntary actions to address social and environmental issues, Shared Value approaches aim to create economic value by addressing societal challenges. By adopting these approaches, companies can enhance their reputation, engage employees, manage risks, access new markets, and contribute to long-term sustainability. Ultimately, embracing CSR and Shared Value is not only beneficial for businesses but also for the well-being of communities and the planet.

Public–Private Partnerships for Market Development

Corporate Social Responsibility (CSR) and Shared Value approaches are two distinct but related concepts that aim to integrate social and environmental considerations into business strategies. Both approaches recognize the importance of businesses taking responsibility for their impact on society and the environment. In this article, we will explore the key principles and benefits of CSR and Shared Value approaches.

Both CSR and Shared Value approaches are valuable frameworks for businesses to contribute positively to society and the environment. While CSR focuses on voluntary actions to address social and environmental issues, Shared Value approaches aim to create economic value by addressing societal challenges. By adopting these approaches, companies can enhance their reputation, engage employees, manage risks, access new markets, and contribute to long-term sustainability. Ultimately, embracing CSR and Shared Value is not only beneficial for businesses but also for the well-being of communities and the planet.

Cross-Sector Collaboration in MSD

The Market System Development (MSD) approach is a comprehensive framework that aims to address complex development challenges by strengthening market systems. A key component of this approach is cross-sector collaboration, which involves the active involvement and coordination of multiple stakeholders from various sectors. In this article, we will explore the importance and benefits of cross-sector collaboration in the Market System Development approach.

Enhanced Knowledge and Expertise: Cross-sector collaboration brings together diverse stakeholders with different areas of expertise and knowledge. By collaborating across sectors such as government, private sector, civil society, and development agencies, the MSD approach can leverage the collective wisdom and experience of these stakeholders. This allows for a more comprehensive understanding of the market system and the challenges it faces, leading to more effective and sustainable interventions. By pooling resources and expertise, cross-sector collaboration enhances the capacity of the MSD approach to address complex development issues.

Holistic and Integrated Approaches: Market systems are complex and interconnected, and their development requires a holistic and integrated approach. Cross-sector collaboration enables the identification and analysis of interdependencies and synergies between different sectors. By working together, stakeholders can develop interventions that consider the broader context and potential impacts on other sectors. This integrated approach ensures that interventions are comprehensive, effective, and sustainable, leading to long-term positive outcomes for the market system and its actors.

Coordinated and Aligned Efforts: Cross-sector collaboration facilitates coordination and alignment of efforts among stakeholders. By working together, stakeholders can avoid duplication of efforts and ensure that resources are utilized efficiently. This collaboration also promotes the sharing of information, data, and best practices, allowing stakeholders to learn from each other and build on existing knowledge. Through coordinated and aligned efforts, cross-sector collaboration maximizes the impact of interventions and enhances the effectiveness of the MSD approach.

Increased Accountability and Ownership: Cross-sector collaboration fosters a sense of accountability and ownership among stakeholders. By involving multiple sectors, the MSD approach encourages stakeholders to take responsibility for their roles and contributions. This accountability promotes transparency, learning, and the sharing of successes and challenges. By working together, stakeholders are more likely to be invested in the outcomes of the interventions and committed to their long-term sustainability.

Leveraging Resources and Networks: Cross-sector collaboration allows for the leveraging of diverse resources and networks. Each sector brings its own resources, networks, and connections to the table, which can be harnessed to support the development of the market system. For example, the private sector may provide financial resources and access to markets, while development agencies may offer technical expertise and capacity-building support. By leveraging these resources and networks, cross-sector collaboration enhances the effectiveness and impact of the interventions.

Policy Coherence and Systemic Change: Cross-sector collaboration contributes to policy coherence and systemic change. By involving stakeholders from different sectors, the MSD approach can address policy constraints and promote policy changes that facilitate market development. This collaboration enables the identification of systemic barriers and the development of strategies to overcome them. By advocating for policy changes and implementing interventions that address systemic issues, cross-sector collaboration drives sustainable and transformative change in the market system.

Cross-sector collaboration is a crucial element of the Market System Development approach. By bringing together stakeholders from different sectors, this collaboration enhances knowledge and expertise, enables holistic and integrated approaches, promotes coordinated and aligned efforts, fosters accountability and ownership, leverages resources and networks, and contributes to policy coherence and systemic change. Through effective cross-sector collaboration, the MSD approach can achieve sustainable and inclusive market development outcomes, benefiting all stakeholders involved.

Collaboration between Government and Civil Society Organizations

Collaboration between government and civil society organizations (CSOs) is a vital component of effective governance and social development. This partnership plays a crucial role in addressing societal challenges, promoting inclusive decision-making, and ensuring the well-being of citizens. In this article, we will explore the importance of collaboration between government and CSOs, the benefits it brings, and examples of successful collaborations.

Importance of Collaboration between Government and CSOs:

Citizen Participation: Collaboration between government and CSOs fosters citizen participation in decision-making processes. CSOs represent the interests and needs of various communities and marginalized groups, ensuring their voices are heard and considered in policy formulation and implementation.

Policy Development and Implementation: CSOs possess valuable expertise and on-the-ground knowledge that can inform policymaking. By collaborating with CSOs, governments can tap into this expertise, ensuring that policies are evidence-based, inclusive, and effective.

Service Delivery and Accountability: CSOs often work closely with communities and provide essential services. Collaboration with government strengthens service delivery mechanisms and ensures accountability for the effective utilization of resources.

Advocacy and Social Justice: CSOs play a crucial role in advocating for the rights of marginalized groups, promoting social justice, and holding governments accountable. Collaboration allows for joint advocacy efforts and the creation of policies that address social inequalities and promote equitable development.

Collaboration between government and CSOs is crucial for effective governance, social development, and the well-being of citizens. By harnessing the expertise, resources, and networks of CSOs, governments can design and implement more inclusive and effective policies. The benefits of collaboration include enhanced policy effectiveness, increased social cohesion, strengthened implementation, innovation, and trust-building. Through successful collaborations, governments and CSOs can work together to address societal challenges, promote social justice, and create a more equitable and sustainable future.

Harmonizing Efforts of Development Practitioners

Harmonizing efforts among development practitioners is crucial for achieving sustainable and impactful development outcomes. In this article, we will explore the concept of harmonizing efforts, its importance in the field of development, and the benefits it brings to practitioners and the communities they serve.

Harmonizing efforts refers to the process of aligning and coordinating the work of various development practitioners, including government agencies, non-governmental organizations (NGOs), international organizations, and other stakeholders. The goal is to ensure that their activities are complementary, mutually reinforcing, and collectively contribute to the overall development objectives.

The benefits of harmonizing efforts extend to both development practitioners and the communities they serve:

- Development practitioners benefit from harmonization by gaining access to additional resources, expertise, and networks. It also reduces competition among practitioners and fosters a collaborative working environment.

- Communities benefit from harmonization as it ensures that interventions are well-coordinated, targeted, and responsive to their needs. Harmonized efforts lead to more comprehensive and sustainable development outcomes that address the root causes of poverty and inequality.

International Cooperation and Funding Mechanisms for MSD

International cooperation and funding mechanisms play a vital role in addressing the challenges related to market systems development (MSD) in developing countries. In this article, we will explore the importance of international cooperation in MSD, the types of funding mechanisms available, and their impact on sustainable development.

Market systems development aims to create an enabling environment that fosters sustainable economic growth and poverty reduction. It involves addressing systemic constraints and market failures that hinder the functioning of markets in developing countries. Given the global nature of these challenges, international cooperation is crucial to effectively tackle them.

International cooperation in MSD involves collaboration among governments, development agencies, multilateral organizations, and other stakeholders. It facilitates the exchange of knowledge, expertise, and resources to strengthen market systems and promote inclusive economic development. Through cooperation, countries can learn from each other's experiences, share best practices, and develop innovative solutions to common challenges.

One important aspect of international cooperation in MSD is the provision of funding mechanisms. These mechanisms aim to mobilize resources and allocate financing to support initiatives that promote market system development. Some common funding mechanisms include:

Official Development Assistance (ODA): ODA refers to financial resources provided by governments of developed countries to support the development efforts of developing countries. ODA can be used to fund various MSD initiatives, such as capacity-building programs, technical assistance, and infrastructure development.

Multilateral Development Banks (MDBs): MDBs, such as the World Bank, Asian Development Bank, and African Development Bank, provide financial support and technical expertise to promote economic development. They offer loans, grants, and technical assistance to finance MSD projects and programs.

Public-Private Partnerships (PPPs): PPPs involve collaboration between public and private entities to address development challenges. In the context of MSD, PPPs can leverage private sector resources and expertise to support market system interventions, such as investment in infrastructure, technology transfer, and skills development.

Impact Investing: Impact investors provide financing to businesses and organizations that generate positive social and environmental outcomes alongside financial returns. Impact investing can play a role in funding MSD initiatives by supporting enterprises that promote inclusive growth and address market failures.

The availability of funding mechanisms for MSD is essential for achieving sustainable development outcomes. These mechanisms provide the necessary financial resources to implement interventions, build local capacities, and address systemic constraints. They also help to leverage additional funding from other sources, such as private sector investment and domestic resources.

International cooperation and funding mechanisms are crucial for promoting market systems development in developing countries. By facilitating collaboration, knowledge exchange, and resource mobilization, international cooperation enables countries to address systemic constraints and promote inclusive economic growth. Funding mechanisms, such as ODA, MDBs, PPPs, and impact investing, play a vital role in providing the necessary financial resources to implement MSD initiatives and achieve sustainable development outcomes. Through effective collaboration and financing, countries can create enabling environments that support vibrant and inclusive market systems, leading to poverty reduction and sustainable development.

Bilateral and Multilateral Aid Agencies in Market Development

Bilateral and multilateral aid agencies play a crucial role in market development efforts around the world. In this article, we will explore the significance of these agencies, their approaches to market development, and the impact they have on economic growth and poverty reduction.

Bilateral aid agencies, also known as donor countries, are government agencies that provide assistance directly to recipient countries. These agencies, such as the United States Agency for International Development (USAID) and the Department for International Development (DFID) in the United Kingdom, have their own development agendas and priorities. Bilateral aid agencies typically provide financial resources, technical expertise, and capacity-building support to recipient countries, with a focus on promoting economic growth and poverty reduction.

Multilateral aid agencies, on the other hand, are international organizations that pool resources from multiple donor countries. Some prominent examples include the World Bank, International Monetary Fund (IMF), and United Nations Development Programme (UNDP). These agencies coordinate efforts among member countries and provide financial resources, technical assistance, and policy advice to support market development initiatives.

Both bilateral and multilateral aid agencies utilize different approaches to market development. Bilateral agencies often tailor their assistance to the specific needs and priorities of recipient countries. They work closely with governments, civil society organizations, and the private sector to design and implement programs that promote inclusive economic growth. Bilateral aid agencies also collaborate with local stakeholders to build capacity, transfer technology, and strengthen institutions.

Multilateral aid agencies, on the other hand, focus on broader development goals and promote global cooperation. They provide financial resources for infrastructure development, policy reforms, and capacity-building initiatives. Multilateral agencies also play a crucial role in coordinating efforts among multiple countries, ensuring effective use of resources, and sharing best practices.

The impact of bilateral and multilateral aid agencies in market development is significant. Their support helps to create an enabling environment for businesses, promote entrepreneurship, and facilitate trade and investment. Aid agencies also assist in improving infrastructure, building human capital, and strengthening institutions, all of which are essential for sustainable market development.

Furthermore, these agencies play a critical role in addressing market failures and systemic constraints that hinder economic growth and poverty reduction. They promote inclusive development by focusing on marginalized populations, supporting women's economic empowerment, and promoting sustainable practices.

Bilateral and multilateral aid agencies are key players in market development efforts. Through their financial resources, technical expertise, and capacity-building support, these agencies contribute to economic growth, poverty reduction, and sustainable development. Their collaborative approach, tailored assistance, and focus on addressing systemic constraints make them indispensable in promoting inclusive and vibrant market systems globally.

Innovative Financing Models for MSD Programs

Innovative financing models have become increasingly important in supporting Market Systems Development (MSD) programs. These models offer new approaches to mobilizing financial resources and ensuring the sustainability and scalability of MSD interventions. In this article, we will explore some of the most notable innovative financing models used in MSD programs and their benefits.

The benefits of these innovative financing models for MSD programs are numerous. They foster greater private sector engagement, mobilize additional financial resources, promote accountability, and encourage innovation. These models also provide opportunities for scaling successful interventions, as they attract investors who are interested in both financial returns and social impact.

Coordinating Donor Support for Market System Transformation

Coordinating donor support is crucial for achieving effective market system transformation. Market system transformation refers to the process of creating sustainable and inclusive market systems that benefit all stakeholders, including producers, consumers, and businesses. In this article, we will explore the importance of coordinating donor support for market system transformation and the key considerations in achieving successful coordination.

Donor coordination plays a vital role in ensuring that resources are allocated efficiently, avoiding duplication of efforts, and maximizing the impact of interventions. When donors coordinate their support for market system transformation, they can pool their resources, expertise, and networks to address common challenges and leverage each other's strengths.

One key consideration in coordinating donor support is alignment with national development priorities and local stakeholders. It is essential to engage with governments, private sector actors, civil society organizations, and other local stakeholders to understand their needs and priorities. By aligning donor support with local contexts, interventions can be tailored to address specific challenges and leverage existing resources and capacities.

Another important consideration is harmonizing approaches and methodologies. Each donor may have their own strategies, methodologies, and indicators for measuring success. Coordinating donor support involves aligning these approaches to ensure consistency and comparability of results. This allows for better monitoring and evaluation of interventions, enabling learning and adaptation throughout the process.

Coordinating donor support also involves sharing knowledge and best practices. Donors can facilitate knowledge exchange platforms, workshops, and learning events where stakeholders can share their experiences, lessons learned, and innovative approaches. This collaboration fosters collective learning and helps to identify effective strategies and interventions for market system transformation.

Lastly, financial coordination is critical in coordinating donor support. It involves aligning funding cycles, reporting requirements, and financial mechanisms to streamline the disbursement and tracking of funds. Financial coordination ensures transparency, accountability, and efficient use of resources.

Coordinating donor support for market system transformation is essential for maximizing the impact of interventions and achieving sustainable and inclusive market systems. By aligning with national priorities, harmonizing approaches, sharing knowledge, and coordinating financial mechanisms, donors can work together to address common challenges and leverage their resources effectively. Coordinated donor support enables efficient allocation of resources, avoids duplication of efforts, and contributes to the overall success of market system transformation initiatives.

Chapter Seven

Scaling up and Replicating Successful MSD Interventions

Scaling up and replicating successful Market Systems Development (MSD) interventions is crucial for achieving sustainable and transformative impact. In this article, we will explore the importance of scaling up and replicating successful MSD interventions and discuss key strategies for effectively expanding their reach.

The Importance of Scaling up and Replicating MSD Interventions

Scaling up successful MSD interventions is essential for maximizing their impact and reaching a larger number of beneficiaries. By scaling up, practitioners can extend the benefits of proven interventions to new geographic areas, sectors, or target groups. Replication, on the other hand, involves implementing the same intervention in different contexts, thereby leveraging the knowledge and experience gained from previous implementations. Scaling up and replicating successful interventions not only accelerates progress towards development goals but also contributes to knowledge sharing and learning within the MSD community.

Strategies for Effective Scaling up and Replication

Document and Share Best Practices: Documenting and sharing best practices is crucial for successful scaling up and replication. MSD practitioners should systematically capture and analyze data, lessons learned, and success stories from their interventions. This information can be disseminated through case studies, reports, conferences, and online platforms, enabling others to learn from and adapt successful interventions.

Strengthen Partnerships and Collaboration: Strong partnerships and collaboration are essential for scaling up and replicating successful MSD interventions. Practitioners should actively engage with stakeholders, including government agencies, donors, NGOs, and private sector actors, to mobilize resources, leverage expertise, and ensure buy-in and support for scaling up efforts. Collaboration can also facilitate the sharing of knowledge, experiences, and networks, enhancing the effectiveness of scaling up and replication initiatives.

Adapt Interventions to Local Contexts: When scaling up or replicating interventions, it is crucial to adapt them to the local context. MSD practitioners should conduct thorough assessments of the new target area or sector, considering cultural, social, economic, and political factors. By tailoring interventions to local realities, practitioners can ensure their relevance, effectiveness, and sustainability.

Build Local Capacity: Building local capacity is key to successful scaling up and replication. MSD practitioners should focus not only on implementing interventions but also on transferring knowledge, skills, and resources to local actors. This can be done through training programs, mentoring, and providing technical assistance. By empowering local actors to take ownership of interventions, practitioners can enhance the sustainability and long-term impact of scaling up and replication efforts.

Monitor, Evaluate, and Learn: Monitoring, evaluating, and learning from scaled-up and replicated interventions is crucial for continuous improvement. MSD practitioners should establish robust monitoring and evaluation systems to track progress, measure impact, and identify areas for refinement. By systematically collecting data and feedback, practitioners can identify what works and what doesn't, enabling them to make informed decisions and adjust strategies accordingly.

Advocate for Policy Change: Scaling up and replicating successful MSD interventions often require supportive policy environments. MSD practitioners should actively engage with policymakers and advocate for policy reforms that can facilitate the expansion of successful interventions. By aligning interventions with national development priorities and promoting enabling policies, practitioners can create an environment conducive to scaling up and replication.

Scaling up MSD programs is essential for achieving widespread impact and transformative change. By building partnerships, adopting adaptive management approaches, leveraging technology, strengthening local capacity, advocating for supportive policies, and promoting knowledge management and learning, practitioners can effectively scale up their programs. These strategies enable the expansion of successful interventions, enhance the reach and impact of MSD programs, and contribute to inclusive and sustainable development.

Identifying Scalable Interventions in Market Systems

Identifying scalable interventions in market systems is crucial for practitioners involved in Market Systems Development (MSD) programs. Scaling up successful interventions allows for broader impact and sustainable development outcomes. In this article, we will explore key strategies for identifying scalable interventions and discuss how practitioners can effectively prioritize and select interventions for expansion.

Importance of Identifying Scalable Interventions

Identifying scalable interventions is essential for maximizing the impact of MSD programs. Scalability refers to the ability of an intervention to be expanded and replicated in different contexts without compromising its effectiveness. By focusing on scalable interventions, practitioners can achieve greater reach, leverage resources more efficiently, and address systemic market failures. Identifying interventions with high scalability potential ensures that limited resources are allocated to initiatives that can generate significant and sustainable impact.

Strategies for Identifying Scalable Interventions

Market Analysis: Conducting a thorough analysis of the market system is the first step in identifying scalable interventions. This involves assessing market dynamics, identifying key actors, understanding supply and demand constraints, and analyzing market failures. By gaining a deep understanding of the market context, practitioners can identify potential entry points for interventions that can lead to systemic change.

Evidence and Data-driven Approach: Utilizing evidence and data to inform decision-making is crucial for identifying scalable interventions. Practitioners should gather and analyze data on the impact, cost-effectiveness, and scalability potential of different interventions. This can be done through rigorous monitoring and evaluation, impact assessments, and research studies. Evidence-basis decision-making ensures that interventions with proven results and scalability are prioritized.

Stakeholder Engagement: Engaging with key stakeholders is vital for identifying scalable interventions. By involving market actors, beneficiaries, government agencies, and other stakeholders in the decision-making process, practitioners can gain insights and perspectives that inform intervention selection. Stakeholder engagement also helps build ownership, foster collaboration, and ensure sustainability.

Systemic Approach: Adopting a systemic approach is essential for identifying scalable interventions. This involves understanding the interdependencies and feedback loops within the market system. By targeting interventions that address underlying market failures rather than focusing on isolated issues, practitioners can achieve sustainable impact and scalability. A systemic approach considers the interactions between different market actors and factors in external influences.

Innovation and Adaptation: Encouraging innovation and adaptation is key to identifying scalable interventions. Practitioners should be open to new ideas, approaches, and technologies that can disrupt existing market systems and lead to positive change. Embracing innovation allows for the exploration of unconventional solutions and the identification of interventions with high scalability potential.

Risk Assessment: Conducting a risk assessment is crucial in identifying scalable interventions. Practitioners should evaluate potential risks and challenges associated with each intervention. This includes assessing financial risks, political risks, market risks, and social risks. By understanding and mitigating these risks, practitioners can prioritize interventions that have a higher likelihood of success and scalability.

Identifying scalable interventions in market systems is a critical step in maximizing the impact of MSD programs. By conducting market analysis, utilizing an evidence and data-driven approach, engaging stakeholders, adopting a systemic perspective, encouraging innovation, and conducting risk assessments, practitioners can effectively identify interventions with high scalability potential. This ensures that resources are allocated to initiatives that can generate significant and sustainable impact, leading to transformative change in market systems and promoting inclusive and sustainable development.

Replication of Successful MSD Models

Replication of successful Market Systems Development (MSD) models is a crucial strategy for achieving scalable and sustainable impact in market development initiatives. By replicating proven models, practitioners can leverage existing knowledge, experiences, and resources to drive positive change in new contexts. In this article, we will explore the importance of replicating successful MSD models, the challenges involved, and strategies for effective replication.

Importance of Replication

Scalability: Replication allows successful MSD models to be expanded to new geographical areas or sectors, reaching a larger number of beneficiaries. This enables the potential for broader economic growth, poverty reduction, and increased resilience within market systems.

Efficiency: Replicating successful models saves time, effort, and resources by building upon existing knowledge and experiences. Lessons learned from previous implementations can be applied to new contexts, streamlining the design and implementation process.

Learning and Adaptation: Through replication, practitioners could learn from both successes and failures. By adapting and refining models based on feedback and lessons learned, practitioners can continually improve and enhance the effectiveness of their interventions.

Evidence-based Approach: Replication of successful MSD models provides evidence of their impact and effectiveness. This evidence can be used to advocate for policy changes, attract funding, and gain support from stakeholders, thereby increasing the chances of achieving sustainable change.

Challenges in Replication

Contextual Adaptation: Successful MSD models may need to be adapted to suit the specific context in which they are being replicated. Factors such as cultural norms, local market dynamics, and regulatory frameworks must be considered. This requires a deep understanding of the new context and careful adaptation of the model without diluting its core principles.

Capacity Building: Replication often involves transferring knowledge and building capacity among local stakeholders. This can be challenging, especially in areas with limited resources and technical expertise. Effective capacity building strategies, including training, mentoring, and knowledge sharing, are crucial for successful replication.

Sustainability: Ensuring the sustainability of replicated models is a key challenge. Replication should include strategies for local ownership, stakeholder engagement, and the establishment of supportive policies and regulations. Sustainable financing mechanisms should also be considered to ensure the longevity of the intervention beyond the initial implementation phase.

Replication of successful MSD models is a powerful strategy for achieving scalable and sustainable impact in market development initiatives. By leveraging existing knowledge, experiences, and resources, practitioners can replicate proven models to drive positive change in new contexts. Overcoming challenges such as contextual adaptation, capacity building, and sustainability requires careful planning, stakeholder engagement, and a flexible approach. With thorough documentation, adaptation, local ownership, monitoring and evaluation, and strong partnerships, effective replication can be achieved, leading to transformative change in market systems.

Documenting and Sharing Best Practices in MSD

Documenting and sharing best practices in Market Systems Development (MSD) is crucial for promoting learning, improving interventions, and driving positive change in market systems. By capturing successful approaches, lessons learned, and innovative strategies, practitioners can contribute to the collective knowledge and enhance the effectiveness of future interventions. In this article, we will explore the importance of documenting and sharing best practices in MSD, the challenges involved, and strategies for effective knowledge management.

Importance of Documentation and Sharing

Learning and Improvement: Documenting best practices allows practitioners to reflect on their experiences, learn from successes and failures, and continuously improve their interventions. By sharing this knowledge, others can benefit from the lessons learned and avoid repeating past mistakes.

Replication and Scaling: Documented best practices serve as a valuable resource for replication and scaling of successful interventions. By sharing detailed information about the design, implementation, and impact of interventions, practitioners can provide guidance and insights to others working in similar contexts.

Evidence-based Decision Making: Documented best practices provide evidence of what works and what doesn't in MSD. This evidence can inform decision-making processes, guide the design of future interventions, and influence policy changes at both local and national levels.

Building a Community of Practice: Sharing best practices fosters collaboration and community building among practitioners. By creating platforms for knowledge sharing, such as conferences, webinars, and online communities, practitioners can connect, learn from each other, and build a collective understanding of effective MSD approaches.

Challenges in Documenting and Sharing

Capturing Tacit Knowledge: Much of the knowledge and expertise in MSD resides in the minds of practitioners. Capturing this tacit knowledge and converting it into explicit documentation can be challenging. Practitioners need to reflect on their experiences, extract key insights, and articulate them in a way that is accessible and understandable to others.

Time and Resource Constraints: Documenting best practices requires time, effort, and resources, which may be limited in many MSD projects. Balancing the need for documentation with the demands of implementation can be challenging. It is important to prioritize knowledge management activities and allocate resources accordingly.

Ensuring Relevance and Applicability: Best practices should be documented in a way that is relevant and applicable to different contexts. Generic templates or guidelines may not be suitable for every situation. Practitioners need to adapt their documentation to the specific needs and constraints of different market systems.

Documenting and sharing best practices in MSD is essential for promoting learning, improving interventions, and driving positive change in market systems. By capturing and sharing experiences, lessons learned, and successful strategies, practitioners can contribute to the collective knowledge and enhance the effectiveness of future interventions. Overcoming challenges such as capturing tacit knowledge and resource constraints requires a systematic approach, stakeholder engagement, and a commitment to continual learning and improvement. By prioritizing documentation, sharing knowledge, and building a community of practice, practitioners can contribute to the growth and development of effective MSD approaches.

Adapting and Customizing MSD Models for Different Contexts

Market Systems Development (MSD) models provide a framework for understanding and addressing bottlenecks and constraints in market systems. However, it is crucial to recognize that a one-size-fits-all approach may not be suitable for every context. Adapting and customizing MSD models is essential to ensure their relevance and effectiveness in different contexts. In this article, we will explore the importance of adapting and customizing MSD models, the factors to consider, and strategies for successful implementation.

Factors to Consider in Adaptation

1) Contextual Analysis: Conduct a thorough analysis of the market system, including its stakeholders, institutions, regulations, and dynamics. Understand the unique characteristics, needs, and challenges of the target market system before designing interventions.
2) Stakeholder Engagement: Engage with a wide range of stakeholders, including market actors, government agencies, and civil society organizations. Involve them in the design and implementation process to ensure their perspectives and knowledge are incorporated into the adapted MSD model.
3) Flexibility and Iteration: Recognize that adaptation is an iterative process. Be prepared to modify and refine

interventions based on feedback, monitoring data, and changing contextual factors. Adaptation should be an ongoing process throughout the implementation of the MSD model.
4) Risk Management: Assess and manage risks associated with adaptation. Understand the potential risks and trade-offs of modifying the MSD model and develop strategies to mitigate these risks. Monitor and evaluate the impact of adaptations to ensure they are achieving the desired outcomes.

Adapting and customizing MSD models is essential for ensuring their relevance, effectiveness, and sustainability in different contexts. By considering contextual factors, engaging stakeholders, and implementing iterative adaptations, practitioners can design interventions that address specific market challenges and opportunities. Successful adaptation requires partnerships, capacity building, learning, and a commitment to monitoring and evaluation. By embracing adaptation, practitioners can enhance the impact and outcomes of MSD interventions and contribute to inclusive and sustainable market systems development.

Promoting South-South Collaboration in Market System Development

Market System Development (MSD) initiatives have traditionally focused on North-South collaborations, where expertise and resources flow from developed countries to developing ones. However, there is increasing recognition of the importance and potential of South-South collaboration in driving inclusive and sustainable market system development. In this article, we will explore the benefits of promoting South-South collaboration in MSD, the key elements for successful collaboration, and examples of initiatives that have successfully implemented this approach.

Benefits of South-South Collaboration

Shared Context and Similar Challenges: South-South collaboration allows for greater understanding and empathy among partner countries. Developing countries often share similar economic, social, and political challenges, making it easier to identify common interests, priorities, and potential solutions. Collaborating with countries facing similar challenges can lead to more relevant and effective interventions.

Knowledge Exchange and Learning: South-South collaboration provides an opportunity for knowledge exchange and learning between countries with similar experiences and contexts. It allows for the sharing of best practices, lessons learned, and innovative approaches to address market system challenges. This exchange of knowledge can lead to more contextually appropriate interventions and accelerate learning and innovation.

Capacity Building and Skill Transfer: South-South collaboration enables the transfer of skills, expertise, and technical knowledge between partner countries. This capacity building approach fosters local ownership, empowerment, and sustainability. By leveraging the strengths and expertise of each partner, countries can develop their own capabilities to drive market system development.

Networking and Regional Integration: South-South collaboration promotes networking and regional integration among partner countries. By working together, countries can establish regional networks, share resources, and develop collective strategies to address common challenges. This collaboration strengthens regional markets, enhances trade, and fosters economic integration.

Key Elements for Successful Collaboration

Shared Vision and Objectives: Establish a shared vision and clear objectives for collaboration. Ensure that all partner countries have a common understanding of the goals, outcomes, and expectations of the collaboration.

Mutual Trust and Respect: Build trust and mutual respect among partner countries. Foster an environment of open communication, transparency, and inclusivity. Recognize and value the unique contributions, perspectives, and expertise of each partner.

Effective Communication and Coordination: Establish effective communication channels and mechanisms for coordination. Regularly exchange information, experiences, and updates to ensure alignment and coordination of activities. Foster a culture of active listening and collaboration.

Resource Sharing and Mutual Support: Promote resource sharing and mutual support among partner countries. Share technical expertise, financial resources, and human capital to support each other's initiatives. Develop mechanisms for resource mobilization and allocation.

Examples of Successful South-South Collaboration Initiatives

Africa Exchange Network (AFEX): AFEX is a collaboration between African countries to promote agricultural market development. It facilitates the exchange of knowledge, experiences, and best practices in agricultural value chain development, trade facilitation, and policy reforms. AFEX has successfully fostered regional integration and enhanced market access for smallholder farmers.

ASEAN Integration Initiative for ASEAN Economic Community (AEC): The ASEAN Integration Initiative promotes economic integration and collaboration among the Southeast Asian countries. It focuses on harmonizing trade policies, facilitating cross-border investments, and promoting regional connectivity. The initiative has led to increased trade, investment flows, and economic cooperation within the ASEAN region.

Latin American and Caribbean Network for Small and Medium Enterprise Development (RED-PYME): RED-PYME is a collaborative platform that promotes the development of small and medium-sized enterprises (SMEs) in Latin America and the Caribbean. It facilitates knowledge exchange, capacity building, and access to finance for SMEs. RED-PYME has contributed to the growth and competitiveness of SMEs in the region.

Promoting South-South collaboration in market system development offers numerous benefits, including shared context and challenges, knowledge exchange, capacity building, and regional integration. By fostering collaboration among developing countries, we can leverage collective expertise, resources, and experiences to drive inclusive and sustainable market system development. Successful collaboration requires shared vision, trust, effective communication, and resource sharing. Initiatives like AFEX, ASEAN Integration Initiative, and RED-PYME serve as inspiring examples of the positive impact of South-South collaboration. By embracing this approach, we can create stronger and more resilient market systems that benefit all participating countries.

Monitoring and Sustaining Market System Transformation

Market system transformation refers to the process of transitioning from traditional market structures to more efficient and inclusive systems. This transformation is crucial for economic development and poverty reduction. However, it is not enough to simply initiate market system transformation; it is equally important to monitor and sustain these changes over time. In this article, we will discuss the significance of monitoring and sustaining market system transformation and explore some strategies to achieve this.

Why Monitor Market System Transformation?

Monitoring market system transformation is essential to ensure that the desired changes are taking place and to identify any gaps or challenges that need to be addressed. It allows policymakers, development practitioners, and other stakeholders to track progress, make informed decisions, and adjust interventions as needed. By monitoring the transformation process, it becomes possible to assess the impact of interventions, identify success stories, and learn from failures.

Monitoring also helps in identifying potential risks and unintended consequences. For example, if a market system transformation leads to job loss or increased inequality, it may be necessary to implement complementary interventions to mitigate these negative effects. Monitoring allows for early detection of such issues and enables proactive measures to be taken.

Strategies for Monitoring and Sustaining Market System Transformation

Establish Baseline Data: Before initiating market system transformation, it is crucial to collect baseline data to establish a benchmark against which progress can be measured. This data should capture relevant indicators such as market structure, competitiveness, access to finance, and the participation of marginalized groups. Regular data collection and analysis will provide insights into the effectiveness of interventions and help in identifying areas that require further attention.

Stakeholder Engagement: Monitoring and sustaining market system transformation require active engagement from various stakeholders, including government agencies, private sector actors, civil society organizations, and local communities. Regular consultations, workshops, and forums should be conducted to gather feedback, share information, and collaborate on sustaining the transformation process.

Continuous Learning and Adaptation: Market system transformation is a dynamic and complex process. It is essential to foster a culture of continuous learning and adaptation to respond to changing circumstances. Regular evaluations and impact assessments should be conducted to identify what works and what doesn't. Based on these findings, interventions can be adjusted or redesigned to ensure sustained progress.

Capacity Building: Strengthening the capacity of individuals and institutions involved in market system transformation is crucial for long-term sustainability. Training programs, workshops, and technical assistance should be provided to enhance the skills and knowledge of stakeholders. This will enable them to effectively monitor, evaluate, and sustain the changes implemented.

Collaboration and Partnerships: Collaboration among different stakeholders is key to sustaining market system transformation. Public-private partnerships, knowledge-sharing platforms, and multi-stakeholder initiatives should be established to foster collaboration and leverage resources and expertise. By working together, stakeholders can pool their resources and efforts to maximize the impact of interventions.

Monitoring and sustaining market system transformation are essential components of successful development initiatives. By monitoring the transformation process, identifying gaps and challenges, and implementing appropriate strategies, policymakers and development practitioners can ensure that the desired changes are achieved and sustained in the long run. Through continuous learning, stakeholder engagement, capacity building, and collaboration, market system transformation can lead to inclusive economic growth, poverty reduction, and improved livelihoods for all.

Long-term Monitoring and Evaluation of MSD Programs

Monitoring and evaluation (M&E) is a critical component of market systems development (MSD) programs. It helps assess the effectiveness, efficiency, and sustainability of interventions and provides valuable insights for program improvement. While short-term monitoring and evaluation efforts are important, the long-term monitoring and evaluation of MSD programs are equally crucial. In this article, we will discuss the significance of long-term M&E in MSD programs and explore some strategies to ensure its effectiveness.

Why is Long-term Monitoring and Evaluation Important?

Long-term monitoring and evaluation provide a comprehensive understanding of the impact and outcomes of MSD programs over an extended period. It helps answer important questions such as whether the desired systemic changes have been achieved, whether there have been unintended consequences, and whether the program has delivered sustainable and lasting results.

Long-term M&E also allows for the identification of trends and patterns that may not be immediately apparent in short-term evaluations. It helps track progress over time, identify barriers and enablers of change, and assess the long-term sustainability of interventions. This information is vital for program managers, policymakers, and funders to make informed decisions, allocate resources effectively, and adjust strategies as needed.

Long-term monitoring and evaluation play a crucial role in assessing the impact and sustainability of MSD programs. By tracking progress, identifying trends, engaging stakeholders, and fostering a culture of learning and adaptation, program managers can ensure that interventions are effective, efficient, and sustainable in the long run. This information is essential for program improvement, resource allocation, and evidence-based decision-making. Ultimately, effective long-term M&E

contributes to the achievement of sustainable and inclusive market systems development.

Ensuring Continuity and Sustainability of Market Changes

Market changes brought about by interventions and programs can have a significant impact on the livelihoods of individuals and the overall economic development of a region. However, ensuring the continuity and sustainability of these market changes is crucial for long-term success. In this article, we will discuss the importance of continuity and sustainability in market changes and explore strategies to achieve them.

Why is Continuity and Sustainability Important?

Continuity and sustainability of market changes ensure that the positive outcomes and benefits of interventions are maintained over time. It is not enough to implement short-term interventions that create temporary improvements. Long-term success requires a focus on creating lasting changes that can withstand external shocks and continue to deliver positive impacts for the target population.

Ensuring the continuity and sustainability of market changes is essential for achieving long-term impact and economic development. By engaging stakeholders, building local capacity, institutionalizing changes, monitoring and evaluating progress, and fostering collaboration, interventions can create lasting transformations in market systems. Continuity and sustainability enable individuals and communities to benefit from improved market conditions, leading to increased incomes, enhanced livelihoods, and sustainable economic growth.

Transferring Ownership to Local Institutions and Stakeholders

Transferring ownership of development initiatives and interventions to local institutions and stakeholders is crucial for ensuring sustainability and long-term impact. It involves empowering local actors to take ownership of programs, projects, and interventions, allowing them to drive and sustain positive change within their communities. In this article, we will explore the importance of transferring ownership to local institutions and stakeholders and discuss strategies to effectively implement this process.

Transferring ownership to local institutions and stakeholders is a key factor in achieving sustainable development outcomes. By empowering local actors, ensuring local relevance, and fostering ownership and responsibility, programs and interventions can have a lasting impact on communities. Through capacity building, participatory approaches, gradual transitions, institutionalization, and ongoing support, ownership transfer becomes a collaborative and empowering process that contributes to sustainable development and positive change.

Chapter Eight

Future Directions and Emerging Trends in MSD

Market System Development (MSD) is an approach that focuses on creating sustainable and inclusive market systems to drive economic development. Over the years, MSD has evolved and adapted to changing dynamics and emerging trends in the global economy. In this article, we will explore the future directions and emerging trends in MSD and their implications for practitioners and stakeholders.

Embracing Digital Transformation: The digital revolution has transformed the way markets operate, and MSD initiatives must adapt to this new reality. The increasing use of technology, such as e-commerce platforms, mobile banking, and digital marketplaces, presents new opportunities for market actors. Future MSD initiatives will need to embrace digital transformation and leverage technology to enhance market linkages, facilitate transactions, and enable access to financial services. This includes promoting digital literacy, building digital infrastructure, and fostering an enabling policy environment for digital innovation.

Addressing Climate Change and Sustainability: As the world faces the challenges of climate change and environmental degradation, MSD initiatives need to prioritize sustainability. Future directions in MSD will focus on promoting environmentally sustainable practices, supporting green entrepreneurship, and encouraging the adoption of renewable energy solutions. MSD practitioners will need to integrate climate change considerations into market assessments, value chain analysis, and intervention design. Collaborating with stakeholders to build resilient and sustainable market systems will be crucial for long-term development.

Promoting Gender Equality and Social Inclusion: Achieving gender equality and social inclusion is a critical aspect of future MSD initiatives. Recognizing the potential of women and marginalized groups as drivers of economic growth, MSD practitioners will need to design interventions that empower these actors. This includes promoting equal access to resources, markets, and opportunities, as well as addressing social and cultural barriers that hinder inclusion. By ensuring that market systems are inclusive and equitable, MSD can contribute to poverty reduction and social development.

Strengthening Collaboration and Partnerships: Future directions in MSD will emphasize the importance of collaboration and partnerships among stakeholders. This includes engaging with governments, private sector actors, civil society organizations, and development agencies. By working together, stakeholders can pool resources, share knowledge, and coordinate efforts to address complex market challenges. Collaboration will also facilitate collective impact and scalability of interventions, ensuring long-term sustainability and systemic change.

Leveraging Data and Analytics: The availability of data and advanced analytics has the potential to revolutionize MSD. Future MSD initiatives will increasingly leverage data to inform decision-making, monitor progress, and evaluate the impact of interventions. Data-driven approaches, such as predictive modeling and machine learning, can provide valuable insights into market dynamics, consumer behavior, and trends. MSD practitioners will need to build capacity in data analysis and use innovative tools to harness the power of data for evidence-based decision-making.

Future directions in Market System Development (MSD) will require practitioners to embrace digital transformation, address climate change and sustainability, promote gender equality and social inclusion, strengthen collaboration and partnerships, and leverage data and analytics. By adapting to emerging trends and embracing new opportunities, MSD can continue to be a powerful approach for driving sustainable and inclusive economic development. As the global landscape evolves, it is essential for MSD practitioners and stakeholders to stay agile, innovative, and responsive to the changing needs of market systems and the communities they serve.

Innovations in Technology and Digital Transformation

Technology and digital transformation have become driving forces in the field of Market System Development (MSD). As markets evolve and adapt to the digital age, incorporating technological innovations into MSD initiatives is essential for sustainable economic growth. In this article, we will explore the innovations in technology and digital transformation that are shaping the future of MSD.

E-commerce Platforms: One of the most significant innovations in technology for MSD is the rise of e-commerce platforms. These platforms enable businesses to reach a broader customer base and facilitate transactions in a more efficient and convenient manner. By leveraging e-commerce platforms, MSD initiatives can support the growth of small businesses, connect them with new markets, and enhance their competitiveness.

Mobile Applications and Payment Systems: Mobile applications and payment systems have revolutionized the way people transact and access financial services. In MSD, the integration of mobile applications and payment systems can enable market actors to conduct business remotely, reach underserved populations, and overcome barriers to financial inclusion. Mobile banking and digital payment solutions can also enhance the efficiency and transparency of value chains, making them more resilient and responsive to market demands.

Internet of Things (IoT): The Internet of Things (IoT) is a network of interconnected devices that can collect and exchange data. In MSD, IoT technology can be used to monitor and optimize various aspects of market systems, such as supply chain logistics, inventory management, and quality control. By capturing real-time data from sensors and devices, MSD practitioners can make informed decisions, identify bottlenecks, and improve the overall efficiency of market operations.

Artificial Intelligence (AI) and Machine Learning (ML): Artificial Intelligence (AI) and Machine Learning (ML) technologies have the potential to transform how MSD initiatives analyze data, predict market trends, and make informed decisions. AI and ML algorithms can process vast amounts of data, identify patterns, and generate actionable insights. This enables MSD practitioners to optimize market interventions, personalize marketing strategies, and improve the effectiveness of value chain management.

Blockchain Technology: Blockchain technology provides a decentralized and transparent platform for secure and efficient transactions. In MSD, blockchain can be used to track and verify the origin and authenticity of products, ensuring fair trade and reducing the risk of fraud. Blockchain-based systems also facilitate trust and collaboration among market actors, enabling more efficient value chain coordination and enhancing market integrity.

Data Analytics and Visualization: The availability of data and advanced analytics tools has opened up new possibilities for MSD. Data analytics and visualization techniques enable practitioners to gain valuable insights into market dynamics, consumer behavior, and performance indicators. By analyzing data, MSD initiatives can identify market gaps, target interventions more effectively, and evaluate the impact of their interventions.

Cloud Computing: Cloud computing has revolutionized the way data is stored, processed, and accessed. In MSD, cloud computing enables practitioners to securely store and share market data, collaborate with stakeholders in real-time, and scale their operations more efficiently. Cloud-based platforms also provide flexibility and cost-effectiveness, allowing MSD initiatives to adapt to changing market needs and resource constraints.

Social media and Digital Marketing: Social media platforms and digital marketing tools have become essential for market actors to reach and engage with their target audience. In MSD, leveraging social media and digital marketing strategies can help businesses promote their products and services, gather customer feedback, and build brand loyalty. This enables market actors to expand their market reach, increase sales, and drive overall market growth.

Technology and digital transformation are driving significant innovations in the field of Market System Development. Incorporating e-commerce platforms, mobile applications, IoT, AI, blockchain, data analytics, cloud computing, and digital marketing into MSD initiatives can enhance market efficiency, inclusivity, and resilience. By embracing these technological advancements, MSD practitioners can unlock new opportunities for sustainable economic growth and create more inclusive and dynamic market systems.

Blockchain and Distributed Ledger Technology in Market Systems

Blockchain and distributed ledger technology (DLT) have shown immense potential in transforming market systems across various industries. These innovative technologies provide secure, transparent, and decentralized solutions that can enhance efficiency, trust, and accountability in market transactions. In the context of market systems, blockchain and DLT offer several key benefits and applications.

Enhanced Transparency and Trust: One of the fundamental features of blockchain and DLT is their ability to provide transparency and trust in market transactions. Through the decentralized nature of these technologies, all participants in a market system can have access to the same information, ensuring transparency and reducing the need for intermediaries. This increased transparency builds trust among participants and minimizes the risk of fraud, counterfeit products, and unethical practices.

Improved Security and Data Integrity: Blockchain and DLT utilize cryptographic techniques to secure data and transactions. Each transaction is recorded in a block, which is linked to the previous block, forming an immutable chain of information. This makes it extremely difficult for malicious actors to alter or tamper with the data. The decentralized nature of these technologies also reduces the risk of a single point of failure, making them highly resilient against cyber-attacks.

Streamlined Supply Chain Management: Blockchain and DLT have the potential to revolutionize supply chain management by providing end-to-end visibility and traceability. With these technologies, each step of the supply chain, from production to distribution, can be recorded in a transparent and immutable manner. This enables stakeholders to track and verify the origin, authenticity, and quality of products, reducing counterfeiting, ensuring compliance with regulations, and improving overall supply chain efficiency.

Efficient Financial Transactions: Blockchain and DLT can streamline financial transactions within market systems by eliminating the need for intermediaries, such as banks or payment processors. Smart contracts, self-executing agreements coded on the blockchain, can automate payment processes, reduce transaction costs, and enable faster settlements. This can be particularly beneficial in cross-border transactions, where traditional banking systems can be slow and costly.

Decentralized Marketplaces: Blockchain and DLT can facilitate the creation of decentralized marketplaces, where buyers and sellers can transact directly without the need for intermediaries. These marketplaces can eliminate barriers to entry, reduce costs, and enable peer-to-peer transactions. By removing intermediaries, blockchain and DLT empower individuals and small businesses, promoting inclusivity and economic empowerment.

Intellectual Property Rights Protection: Blockchain and DLT can offer robust solutions for protecting intellectual property rights in market systems. These technologies can create a decentralized and immutable ledger of copyrights, patents, and trademarks, ensuring that ownership and rights are securely recorded and verified. This can help prevent intellectual property infringement and enable creators and innovators to protect and monetize their creations effectively.

Tokenization and Crowdfunding: Blockchain and DLT enable the tokenization of assets, allowing fractional ownership and facilitating crowdfunding. By representing physical or digital assets as tokens on the blockchain, individuals can buy, sell, and trade these assets with ease. This opens new avenues for fundraising, investment, and liquidity in market systems, democratizing access to capital and creating opportunities for innovation.

Blockchain and distributed ledger technology have the potential to revolutionize market systems by enhancing transparency, trust, security, and efficiency. These technologies offer a wide range of applications, including supply chain management, financial transactions, decentralized marketplaces, intellectual property rights protection, and tokenization. As blockchain and DLT continue to evolve, their adoption in market systems is likely to increase, bringing about transformative changes and unlocking new opportunities for businesses and individuals alike.

Artificial Intelligence and Data Analytics for Market Development

Artificial intelligence (AI) and data analytics have emerged as powerful tools in the realm of market systems development (MSD). These technologies offer unique capabilities to analyze vast amounts of data, gain valuable insights, and drive informed decision-making. In the context of MSD, AI and data analytics play a crucial role in understanding market dynamics, identifying trends, and designing effective interventions.

Data-Driven Decision Making: AI and data analytics enable market development practitioners to make data-driven decisions. By harnessing the power of machine learning algorithms and statistical models, these technologies can process and analyze large datasets to identify patterns, correlations, and trends. This information can be used to inform strategies, policies, and interventions that address specific market challenges and opportunities.

Market Intelligence and Research: AI and data analytics provide valuable tools for market intelligence and research. Through the analysis of market data, including customer preferences, competitor behaviors, and economic indicators, practitioners can gain a comprehensive understanding of market dynamics. This knowledge can guide the development of effective market assessments, feasibility studies, and market entry strategies.

Targeted Interventions: AI and data analytics enable practitioners to identify specific market segments and customer needs. By analyzing customer behavior, purchasing patterns, and demographic data, practitioners can develop targeted interventions that address the specific needs and preferences of different customer groups. This approach increases the effectiveness and efficiency of interventions, leading to better outcomes in market development initiatives.

Predictive Analytics: AI and data analytics can leverage historical data to make predictions about future market trends and behaviors. By analyzing historical sales data, market trends, and external factors, practitioners can develop predictive models that forecast market demand, customer behavior, and supply chain dynamics. These insights enable practitioners to proactively respond to market changes and anticipate future challenges and opportunities.

Automation and Efficiency: AI and data analytics can automate repetitive tasks and processes, improving efficiency in market development initiatives. By leveraging AI-powered algorithms, practitioners can automate data collection, analysis, and reporting, freeing up valuable time for more strategic decision-making and intervention design. This automation reduces human error, increases productivity, and allows practitioners to focus on high-value activities.

Risk Assessment and Mitigation: AI and data analytics can assess and mitigate risks in market systems. By analyzing historical data, market trends, and external factors, practitioners can identify potential risks, such as market volatility, supply chain disruptions, or regulatory changes. This information allows practitioners to develop risk management strategies and contingency plans to mitigate the impact of these risks on market development initiatives.

Continuous Monitoring and Evaluation: AI and data analytics enable practitioners to continuously monitor and evaluate the impact of market development interventions. By collecting and analyzing real-time data, practitioners can assess the effectiveness and efficiency of interventions, identify areas for improvement, and make data-driven adjustments to intervention strategies. This iterative approach enhances the learning process and ensures that interventions are responsive to changing market dynamics.

AI and data analytics hold tremendous potential for market developments. These technologies enable practitioners to make data-driven decisions, gain market intelligence, develop targeted interventions, and predict market trends. They also automate tasks, assess and mitigate risks, and enable continuous monitoring and evaluation. As AI and data analytics continue to advance, their integration into MSD practices will play a pivotal role in driving positive and sustainable market outcomes.

Fine-tech and Digital Financial Inclusion in MSD

Fintech, or financial technology, has revolutionized the way financial services are accessed and delivered, particularly in the context of market systems development (MSD). Fintech solutions have the potential to drive digital financial inclusion, empowering individuals and businesses with access to affordable and convenient financial services.

In the realm of MSD, fintech plays a crucial role in expanding financial inclusion, promoting economic growth, and fostering sustainable development.

Digital Payments and Mobile Money: Fintech has facilitated the rise of digital payments and mobile money solutions, which have transformed the way financial transactions are conducted. In MSD, these technologies enable individuals and businesses in underserved areas to access and use financial services, such as making payments, transferring money, and receiving funds. Digital payments and mobile money solutions provide a safe, convenient, and cost-effective alternative to traditional banking services, especially for populations with limited access to formal financial institutions.

Access to Credit and Financing: Fintech platforms have opened new avenues for accessing credit and financing, particularly for small and medium-sized enterprises (SMEs) in MSD. Through digital lending platforms, SMEs can access loans and capital without the need for extensive paperwork or collateral requirements. Fintech solutions use alternative data sources and innovative credit scoring models to assess creditworthiness, enabling previously underserved businesses to obtain the financing they need to grow and thrive.

Financial Literacy and Education: Fintech plays a vital role in promoting financial literacy and education, which are essential components of digital financial inclusion. Through mobile applications, online platforms, and digital tools, fintech solutions provide individuals with access to financial education resources, budgeting tools, and personalized financial advice. By improving financial literacy, individuals are empowered to make informed financial decisions, engage with formal financial services, and build a foundation for long-term financial stability.

Insurance and Risk Management: Fintech innovations have also enhanced access to insurance and risk management solutions in MSD. Through digital insurance platforms, individuals and businesses can access affordable and customized insurance products that protect against various risks, such as crop failure, natural disasters, or health emergencies. Fintech solutions leverage data analytics and advanced algorithms to streamline the insurance process, reduce administrative costs, and expand the reach of insurance services to previously underserved populations.

Digital Identity and KYC: Fintech solutions are instrumental in overcoming challenges related to identification and Know Your Customer (KYC) requirements in MSD. Through digital identity verification systems, individuals can establish their identity using biometric data or other secure digital means. This enables them to access financial services, open bank accounts, and participate in formal economic activities. Digital identity solutions enhance security, reduce fraud, and facilitate greater financial inclusion by eliminating the need for physical documentation and in-person verification.

Partnerships and Collaboration: Fintech companies often collaborate with traditional financial institutions, non-governmental organizations (NGOs), and government agencies to drive digital financial inclusion in MSD. These partnerships leverage the strengths of each stakeholder to create innovative solutions, expand outreach, and ensure the sustainability of fintech initiatives. By working together, fintech providers and development actors can address regulatory challenges, build trust, and create an enabling environment for digital financial inclusion to thrive.

Data Analytics and Market Insights: Fintech solutions generate vast amounts of data, which can be harnessed for data analytics and market insights in MSD. By analyzing transactional data, customer behavior, and market trends, fintech platforms can provide valuable insights to inform intervention design, market assessments, and policy-making. These data-driven insights enable practitioners to make informed decisions, target interventions effectively, and monitor the impact of financial inclusion initiatives.

Fine-tech has the potential to drive digital financial inclusion in the context of MSD. By leveraging digital payments, digital lending, financial education, insurance, digital identity, and partnerships, fintech solutions can overcome barriers to financial inclusion and empower individuals and businesses with access to affordable and convenient financial services. As the fintech landscape continues to evolve, its integration into MSD practices will play a pivotal role in promoting economic growth, poverty reduction, and sustainable development.

Climate Change and Resilience in Market Systems

Climate change poses significant challenges to market systems development (MSD) efforts worldwide. The increasing frequency and intensity of extreme weather events, rising sea levels, and changing precipitation patterns impact the functioning of markets, livelihoods, and economic activities. In this context, building resilience within market systems becomes essential for ensuring sustainable development and addressing the adverse effects of climate change.

Understanding Climate Risks: To enhance resilience in market systems, it is crucial to understand the specific climate risks and their potential impacts on various sectors and value chains. This involves conducting comprehensive climate risk assessments, analyzing vulnerabilities, and identifying adaptation measures. By understanding the climate risks, market actors can proactively develop strategies to mitigate and adapt to the changing environmental conditions.

Diversification and Adaptation: Market systems need to diversify their activities and adapt to changing climate conditions to remain resilient. This may involve diversifying income sources, shifting production practices, adopting climate-smart technologies, and promoting sustainable agricultural practices. By diversifying their activities, market actors can reduce their dependence on climate-sensitive sectors and enhance their ability to withstand shocks and disruptions caused by climate change.

Access to Climate Finance: Access to climate finance is vital for strengthening resilience in market systems. Climate finance can support the implementation of adaptation and mitigation measures, promote sustainable practices, and facilitate the transition to low-carbon economies. Through partnerships with financial institutions, development agencies, and private sector actors, market systems can access the necessary funding to build climate resilience and foster sustainable development.

Strengthening Value Chains: Resilient market systems require robust and adaptive value chains. This involves enhancing the resilience of key market actors, such as producers, processors, distributors, and retailers, to climate-related risks. By improving infrastructure, strengthening supply chains, and promoting efficient logistics, market systems can adapt to changing conditions and ensure the smooth flow of goods and services even in the face of climate-related disruptions.

Knowledge Sharing and Capacity Building: Building resilience in market systems necessitates knowledge sharing and capacity building initiatives. This involves providing training and technical assistance to market actors on climate-smart practices, risk management strategies, and adaptation measures. By equipping market actors with the necessary knowledge and skills, they can make informed decisions, implement climate-resilient practices, and effectively respond to climate-related challenges.

Stakeholder Collaboration: Collaboration among various stakeholders is crucial for enhancing resilience in market systems. This includes partnerships between governments, NGOs, private sector entities, and local communities. By working together, these stakeholders can coordinate efforts, share resources, and leverage their respective expertise to build climate resilience at the system level. Collaborative initiatives can include the development of climate-smart policies, the establishment of early warning systems, and the implementation of adaptation and mitigation strategies.

Policy and Regulatory Support: Governments play a critical role in fostering climate resilience in market systems through supportive policies and regulations. This includes incentivizing climate-smart practices, promoting sustainable investments, and integrating climate considerations into national development plans. By creating an enabling environment, governments can encourage market actors to adopt resilient practices, invest in climate-friendly technologies, and contribute to the overall resilience of the market system.

Climate change poses significant challenges to market systems development. However, by understanding climate risks, diversifying and adapting, accessing climate finance, strengthening value chains, promoting knowledge sharing and capacity building, fostering stakeholder collaboration, and providing policy support, market systems can enhance their resilience and effectively navigate the impacts of climate change. Building climate resilience in market systems is not only essential for ensuring sustainable development but also for safeguarding livelihoods, promoting economic growth, and creating a more resilient future for all.

Adapting Market Systems to Climate Change Impacts

Climate change presents significant challenges to market systems around the world. As temperatures rise, extreme weather events become more frequent, and natural resources deplete, the way we produce, distribute, and consume goods and services must adapt to mitigate the impacts of climate change. In this article, we will explore the need for adapting market systems to climate change impacts and discuss some key strategies and initiatives that can help address these challenges.

Understanding the Need for Adaptation: Climate change affects market systems in various ways. Rising temperatures can disrupt agricultural production, leading to food shortages and price volatility. Extreme weather events, such as hurricanes and floods, can damage infrastructure and disrupt supply chains. Changes in precipitation patterns can affect water availability, impacting industries such as energy, manufacturing, and tourism. It is crucial to understand these impacts and take proactive measures to adapt market systems to ensure their resilience.

Building Resilient Supply Chains: One key strategy for adapting market systems to climate change impacts is building resilient supply chains. This involves identifying vulnerabilities and implementing measures to reduce risk. For example, companies can diversify their sourcing locations to minimize the impact of extreme weather events in a particular region. They can also invest in technology and infrastructure that can withstand climate-related hazards. Collaborative efforts between businesses, governments, and communities are essential to ensure the resilience of supply chains.

Promoting Sustainable Agriculture and Production: Agriculture is highly vulnerable to climate change impacts. Rising temperatures, changes in rainfall patterns, and the spread of pests and diseases pose significant challenges to farmers and food producers. To adapt, market systems need to promote sustainable agriculture practices such as agroforestry, organic farming, and precision agriculture. These practices can help conserve natural resources, improve soil health, and enhance the resilience of crops to climate-related stresses.

Encouraging Green Innovation and Technology: Innovation and technology play a crucial role in adapting market systems to climate change impacts. Green technologies, such as renewable energy sources and energy-efficient solutions, can reduce greenhouse gas emissions and mitigate the effects of climate change. Governments and businesses should support research and development in these areas and provide incentives for the adoption of green technologies. Promoting innovation and technology transfer can drive sustainable economic growth while reducing the carbon footprint of market systems.

Enhancing Financial Mechanisms: Adapting market systems to climate change impacts requires significant investments. Governments, financial institutions, and development organizations need to develop and enhance financial mechanisms to support adaptation efforts. This can include providing low-interest loans, grants, and insurance options for businesses and communities affected by climate change. Access to finance is critical for implementing adaptation strategies and ensuring the long-term viability of market systems.

Adapting market systems to climate change impacts is a crucial step in building resilience and ensuring long-term sustainability. By understanding the need for adaptation, building resilient supply chains, promoting sustainable agriculture and production, encouraging green innovation and technology, and enhancing financial mechanisms, we can create market systems that can withstand the challenges posed by climate change. Collaboration between stakeholders at all levels is vital to drive these adaptation efforts and secure a sustainable future for our economies and communities.

Promoting Climate-Smart Agriculture and Renewable Energy Markets

As the impacts of climate change become increasingly evident, it is crucial to promote climate-smart agriculture and renewable energy markets as part of sustainable development strategies. Climate-smart agriculture focuses on practices that increase productivity, enhance resilience to climate change, and reduce greenhouse gas emissions. Renewable energy markets aim to transition away from fossil fuels and promote the use of clean, sustainable energy sources. In this article, we will explore the importance of promoting climate-smart agriculture and renewable energy markets and discuss the benefits and challenges associated with these initiatives.

Climate-Smart Agriculture: Climate-smart agriculture involves implementing practices that help mitigate and adapt to climate change while ensuring food security and sustainable livelihoods for farmers. Some key strategies include:

a. *Conservation agriculture*: This approach involves minimizing soil disturbance, maintaining soil cover, and crop rotation to enhance soil health and moisture retention.
b. *Agroforestry*: Integrating trees with crops and livestock can provide multiple benefits, such as carbon sequestration, biodiversity conservation, and improved water management.
c. *Precision farming*: Using technology, such as remote sensing and precision irrigation, can optimize resource use, reduce input costs, and minimize environmental impact.
d. *Climate-resilient crop varieties*: Developing and promoting crop varieties that are more tolerant to heat, drought, pests, and diseases can enhance agricultural productivity in the face of climate change.

By promoting climate-smart agriculture, we can improve food security, enhance farmer resilience, and reduce greenhouse gas emissions from the agricultural sector.

Renewable Energy Markets: Renewable energy markets play a critical role in transitioning away from fossil fuels and reducing greenhouse gas emissions. Renewable energy sources, such as solar, wind, hydro, and geothermal power, offer sustainable alternatives to traditional energy sources. Some key benefits of promoting renewable energy markets include:

a. *Climate mitigation*: Renewable energy sources produce little to no greenhouse gas emissions, helping to reduce the carbon footprint and mitigate climate change.
b. *Energy security*: Diversifying energy sources through renewables reduces dependence on fossil fuels and enhances energy security.
c. *Job creation*: The renewable energy sector has the potential to create numerous jobs, driving economic growth and promoting sustainable development.
d. *Improved air quality*: Unlike fossil fuels, renewable energy sources do not emit pollutants that contribute to air pollution and respiratory illnesses.

However, promoting renewable energy markets also comes with challenges, such as high upfront costs, intermittency issues, and the need for supportive policies and infrastructure.

Synergies between Climate-Smart Agriculture and Renewable Energy: There are significant synergies between climate-smart agriculture and renewable energy markets. For example:

a. *Bioenergy*: Certain crops, residues, and waste products can be used to produce bioenergy, providing a renewable energy source while promoting sustainable agriculture practices.
b. *Solar-powered irrigation*: Installing solar panels to power irrigation systems can enhance water efficiency in agriculture while utilizing clean energy sources.
c. *Agrivoltaics*: Combining solar panels with agricultural activities, such as growing crops or raising livestock, maximizes land use efficiency and promotes both renewable energy generation and sustainable agriculture.

By promoting these synergies, we can create integrated systems that contribute to climate change mitigation, sustainable agriculture, and renewable energy production. Promoting climate-smart agriculture and renewable energy markets is essential for mitigating climate change, ensuring food security, enhancing energy security, and driving sustainable development. By implementing climate-smart agricultural practices and transitioning to renewable energy sources, we can create a more resilient, low-carbon future. However, it is crucial to address the challenges associated with these initiatives through supportive policies, investments in research and development, and collaboration between stakeholders at all levels.

Building Resilience in Vulnerable Communities through MSD

In the face of various challenges, vulnerable communities around the world often struggle to cope with the impacts of poverty, inequality, conflict, and climate change.

To address these complex issues, a multidimensional approach called Market Systems Development (MSD) has emerged as a powerful tool for building resilience in these communities. MSD focuses on strengthening market systems to create sustainable opportunities for economic growth and social development. In this article, we will explore the importance of building resilience in vulnerable communities through MSD and discuss the benefits and challenges associated with this approach.

By adopting an MSD approach, vulnerable communities can build resilience by strengthening their economic systems and improving their ability to adapt to shocks and stresses.

Benefits of Building Resilience through MSD:

Poverty reduction: By strengthening market systems, MSD can create economic opportunities for vulnerable communities, leading to increased incomes and improved livelihoods.

Inclusive growth: MSD aims to ensure that the benefits of economic growth are shared equitably, promoting social inclusion and reducing inequality.

Empowerment: By engaging with market actors and fostering their capacity, MSD enables communities to take ownership of their development processes and make informed decisions.

Risk reduction: Building resilience through MSD helps communities better anticipate and respond to shocks and stresses, reducing their vulnerability to future crises.

Sustainable development: MSD promotes environmentally sustainable practices, such as resource-efficient production methods and the adoption of clean technologies.

Challenges and Considerations

While MSD offers significant potential, it also presents challenges that need to be addressed:

Complex systems: Market systems are intricate and influenced by various factors, requiring a deep understanding of local contexts and dynamics.

Stakeholder coordination: Effective MSD implementation requires collaboration and coordination among diverse stakeholders, including government agencies, NGOs, and private sector actors.

Long-term commitment: Building resilience through MSD is a long-term process that requires sustained investment, patience, and flexibility.

Risk of unintended consequences: MSD interventions must be carefully designed and monitored to avoid unintended negative impacts on vulnerable populations.

Addressing these challenges requires a comprehensive approach, involving rigorous analysis, stakeholder engagement, adaptive management, and learning from both successes and failures.

Building resilience in vulnerable communities through MSD is vital for promoting sustainable development, poverty reduction, and social inclusion. By strengthening market systems and empowering communities, MSD enables them to adapt, thrive, and withstand future challenges. However, it is crucial to recognize the complexity of market systems and the need for long-term commitment and collaboration. By adopting an inclusive and adaptive approach, we can foster resilience in vulnerable communities, creating a brighter and more equitable future for all.

Addressing Inequality and Social Inclusion in MSD

Market Systems Development (MSD) has gained recognition as an effective approach for promoting economic growth and poverty reduction. However, it is crucial to ensure that the benefits of MSD interventions are equitably distributed and inclusive of all members of society. Addressing inequality and promoting social inclusion within the context of MSD is essential for creating sustainable and transformative change. In this article, we will explore the importance of addressing inequality and social inclusion in MSD and discuss strategies to achieve these goals.

Understanding Inequality in the Context of MSD

Inequality refers to the unequal distribution of resources, opportunities, and benefits within a society. Within the market systems framework, inequalities can manifest in various ways, including unequal access to markets, limited participation of marginalized groups, and disparities in income and wealth. Addressing these inequalities is crucial for ensuring that the benefits of market development are shared equitably.

Promoting Social Inclusion in MSD

Social inclusion is about ensuring that all individuals and groups have equal opportunities to participate in and benefit from market systems. It involves addressing barriers and biases that prevent marginalized and vulnerable populations from fully participating in economic activities. Here are some strategies to promote social inclusion in MSD:

Inclusive market assessments: Conducting comprehensive market assessments that consider the needs, constraints, and capacities of marginalized groups. This helps identify barriers to their participation and informs the design of targeted interventions.

Stakeholder engagement: Actively involving marginalized groups, including women, ethnic minorities, persons with disabilities, and youth, in decision-making processes. Their participation ensures that their voices are heard, their needs are addressed, and their perspectives are incorporated into interventions.

Capacity building: Providing targeted training and support to marginalized groups to enhance their skills, knowledge, and confidence to participate effectively in market activities. This may include entrepreneurship training, vocational skills development, and financial literacy programs.

Access to finance and resources: Facilitating access to credit, financial services, and productive resources for marginalized groups. This can be achieved through innovative financial solutions, microfinance programs, and inclusive value chain development.

Gender mainstreaming: Recognizing and addressing gender inequalities within market systems. This involves promoting women's economic empowerment, addressing gender-based discrimination, and ensuring equal access to resources and opportunities.

Monitoring and Evaluation for Social Inclusion

Monitoring and evaluation (M&E) play a critical role in ensuring that social inclusion objectives are met within MSD interventions. M&E frameworks should incorporate indicators related to social inclusion and measure progress in reaching marginalized groups. Regular data collection and analysis can help identify gaps, assess the impact of interventions, and inform adaptive management strategies.

Collaboration and Partnerships

Addressing inequality and social inclusion requires collaboration among various stakeholders, including government agencies, civil society organizations, private sector actors, and marginalized communities themselves. Partnerships can leverage resources, expertise, and networks to design and implement inclusive interventions. It is essential to engage in meaningful and respectful collaborations that prioritize the needs and aspirations of marginalized groups.

addressing inequality and promoting social inclusion within the context of MSD is crucial for creating sustainable and transformative change. By adopting inclusive strategies, engaging marginalized groups, and promoting equitable access to resources and opportunities, MSD can contribute to reducing inequality and building more inclusive market systems. Through collaborative efforts, we can strive for a society where everyone has equal opportunities to participate in and benefit from economic development.

Gender Mainstreaming and Women's Economic Empowerment

In the field of Market Systems Development (MSD), gender mainstreaming and women's economic empowerment have emerged as key areas of focus. Recognizing the importance of gender equality and women's empowerment in driving sustainable development, efforts are being made to integrate a gender perspective into MSD interventions. This article explores the significance of gender mainstreaming and women's economic empowerment within the context of MSD, highlighting their benefits and outlining strategies to achieve these goals.

Gender Mainstreaming in MSD

Gender mainstreaming refers to the integration of a gender perspective into all aspects of policy, planning, and programming. In the context of MSD, this means considering the different needs, roles, and opportunities of women and men within market systems. By mainstreaming gender, it becomes possible to identify and address the barriers that prevent women from fully participating in economic activities and benefiting from market development initiatives.

Importance of Women's Economic Empowerment

Women's economic empowerment is a critical component of gender mainstreaming in MSD. When women are empowered economically, they have greater control over resources, increased access to financial services, and improved livelihood opportunities. This leads to more inclusive and sustainable economic growth. Women's economic empowerment has positive ripple effects on their families, communities, and the overall economy.

Strategies for Gender Mainstreaming and Women's Economic Empowerment in MSD

Gender-responsive market assessments: Conducting market assessments that specifically consider the needs, constraints, and opportunities for women. This helps in identifying gender-based inequalities and designing interventions that address these disparities.

Capacity building for women: Providing targeted training and support to enhance women's skills, knowledge, and confidence in participating in market activities. This may include entrepreneurship training, financial literacy programs, and leadership development initiatives.

Access to finance and assets: Facilitating women's access to financial services, credit, and productive assets. This can be achieved through inclusive financial products, microfinance programs, and initiatives that promote women's property rights.

Gender-inclusive value chain development: Ensuring that women are included at every stage of the value chain, from production to marketing and distribution. This involves addressing gender-based constraints in accessing inputs, technology, and market information.

Promoting women's leadership and decision-making: Creating opportunities for women to participate in decision-making processes related to market systems development. This includes involving women in planning, policy formulation, and representation in relevant forums.

Engaging men and changing social norms: Recognizing the importance of engaging men as allies in promoting gender equality. Efforts should be made to challenge and transform harmful social norms and stereotypes that perpetuate gender inequalities.

Monitoring and Evaluation for Gender Mainstreaming

Monitoring and evaluation (M&E) play a crucial role in ensuring that gender mainstreaming objectives are met within MSD interventions. M&E frameworks should incorporate gender-responsive indicators, collect sex-disaggregated data, and measure progress in women's economic empowerment. Regular data collection and analysis can help identify gaps, assess the impact of interventions, and inform adaptive management strategies.

Gender mainstreaming and women's economic empowerment are essential aspects of Market Systems Development. By integrating a gender perspective into MSD interventions and promoting women's economic empowerment, we can foster more inclusive and sustainable market systems. Through targeted strategies, capacity building, and inclusive policies, we can create an enabling environment where women have equal opportunities to participate in and benefit from economic activities, contributing to overall economic growth and development.

Inclusive Business Models and Disability-Inclusive Market Systems

In the realm of Market Systems Development (MSD), inclusive business models and disability-inclusive market systems have gained significant attention. Recognizing the importance of inclusivity and accessibility, efforts are being made to create market systems that cater to the needs and rights of persons with disabilities. This article explores the significance of inclusive business models and disability-inclusive market systems within the context of MSD, highlighting their benefits and outlining strategies to achieve these goals.

Inclusive Business Models in MSD:

Inclusive business models refer to approaches that aim to include marginalized and underrepresented groups, such as persons with disabilities, in market activities. In the context of MSD, inclusive business models focus on creating economic opportunities for persons with disabilities and ensuring their full and equal participation in market systems. By incorporating inclusive practices, businesses can tap into the potential of this untapped market segment, while also promoting social inclusion and diversity.

Importance of Disability-Inclusive Market Systems:

Disability-inclusive market systems are crucial for

promoting the rights and economic empowerment of persons with disabilities. When market systems are designed to be inclusive, persons with disabilities have equal access to resources, services, and opportunities. This not only enhances their economic well-being but also contributes to social inclusion and reduces poverty and inequality.

Strategies for Inclusive Business Models and Disability-Inclusive Market Systems in MSD:

Accessibility and Universal Design: Ensuring that market infrastructure, products, and services are accessible to persons with disabilities. This includes providing physical accessibility, developing inclusive communication channels, and incorporating universal design principles into product development.

Disability-Inclusive Value Chains: Promoting the inclusion of persons with disabilities in every stage of the value chain, from production to distribution. This involves addressing barriers and providing support for disability-owned businesses, accessible transportation, and inclusive procurement practices.

Skills Development and Capacity Building: Providing training and skill development opportunities for persons with disabilities to enhance their employability and entrepreneurship skills. This includes offering vocational training, mentorship programs, and inclusive workplace practices.

a. *Access to Finance*: Facilitating access to financial services and credit for persons with disabilities to start or expand their businesses. This can be achieved through targeted financial products, inclusive lending practices, and partnerships between financial institutions and disability organizations.

b. *Policy and Advocacy*: Advocating for disability-inclusive policies and regulations that promote the rights and economic inclusion of persons with disabilities. This includes engaging with policymakers, raising awareness, and promoting the implementation of international standards, such as the United Nations Convention on the Rights of Persons with Disabilities.

Monitoring and Evaluation for Inclusive Business Models

Monitoring and evaluation (M&E) are essential for assessing the effectiveness of inclusive business models and disability-inclusive market systems in MSD. M&E frameworks should incorporate indicators that measure the inclusion and economic empowerment of persons with disabilities. Regular data collection and analysis can help identify gaps, measure impact, and inform adaptive strategies to ensure continuous improvement.

Inclusive business models and disability-inclusive market systems are integral to Market Systems Development. By incorporating inclusive practices, promoting accessibility, and addressing barriers, we can create market systems that empower persons with disabilities and promote their full participation in economic activities. Through targeted strategies, capacity building, and policy advocacy, we can foster an environment where everyone, regardless of their abilities, has equal opportunities to thrive and contribute to inclusive and sustainable economic growth.

Promoting Youth Entrepreneurship and Employment in Markets

Within the realm of Market Systems Development (MSD), promoting youth entrepreneurship and employment has become a crucial focus. Recognizing the importance of empowering the youth and creating opportunities for them in the market, efforts are being made to foster an environment that supports their entrepreneurial aspirations and enhances their employability. This article explores the significance of promoting youth entrepreneurship and employment within the context of MSD, highlighting the benefits and outlining strategies to achieve these goals.

Importance of Youth Entrepreneurship and Employment in Markets: Youth entrepreneurship and employment are vital for inclusive economic growth, poverty reduction, and sustainable development. By promoting entrepreneurship among young individuals, we can nurture innovation, create job opportunities, and enhance economic resilience. Additionally, youth employment ensures that young people have access to decent work and can contribute to their communities, while also fostering social inclusion and reducing the risk of social unrest.

Strategies for Promoting Youth Entrepreneurship and Employment in Markets:

Entrepreneurship Education and Training: Providing young individuals with access to entrepreneurship education and training programs. This includes equipping them with the necessary knowledge, skills, and tools to start and manage their businesses successfully. Entrepreneurship education can be integrated into formal education systems and supplemented with practical training and mentorship opportunities.

Access to Finance and Business Support Services: Facilitating access to finance for young entrepreneurs through targeted financial products and services. This includes microcredit, grants, and venture capital funds specifically designed for youth-led businesses. Additionally, providing business support services such as incubators, accelerators, and mentorship programs can help young entrepreneurs navigate the challenges of starting and scaling their ventures.

Creating a Supportive Entrepreneurial Ecosystem: Fostering an enabling environment for youth entrepreneurship by addressing regulatory barriers and creating supportive policies. This includes streamlining business registration processes, reducing bureaucratic hurdles, and implementing youth-friendly policies that incentivize entrepreneurship.

Skills Development and Vocational Training: Enhancing the employability of young individuals by providing them with relevant skills and vocational training.

This can be achieved through partnerships between educational institutions, private sector organizations, and government agencies. The training should align with market demands and equip youth with skills that are in high demand in the job market.

Networking and Collaboration Opportunities: Facilitating networking and collaboration among young entrepreneurs through platforms such as entrepreneurship networks, industry associations, and business incubators. Providing opportunities for young entrepreneurs to connect, learn from each other, and access mentorship can significantly enhance their chances of success.

Monitoring and Evaluation for Youth Entrepreneurship and Employment

Monitoring and evaluation (M&E) play a vital role in assessing the effectiveness of interventions aimed at promoting youth entrepreneurship and employment. M&E frameworks should incorporate indicators that measure the number of youth entrepreneurs supported, jobs created, and the impact on economic growth and social inclusion. Regular data collection and analysis can help identify gaps, measure impact, and inform evidence-based decision-making.

Promoting youth entrepreneurship and employment is essential for inclusive economic growth and sustainable development. By providing young individuals with the necessary skills, access to finance, and a supportive entrepreneurial ecosystem, we can unlock their potential and empower them to contribute meaningfully to the market. Through targeted strategies, collaboration, and continuous monitoring and evaluation, we can create an environment that nurtures youth entrepreneurship and enhances youth employment, paving the way for a prosperous future for both individuals and communities.

Chapter Nine

Application Areas of Market System Development Approach

The Market System Development (MSD) approach is a holistic and inclusive framework that aims to promote sustainable economic growth and poverty reduction. It focuses on improving the functioning of market systems to create opportunities for all market actors, particularly those living in poverty. In this article, we will explore the various application areas of the Market System Development approach and understand how it can be implemented to address different development challenges.

Agriculture and Rural Development: Agriculture is a crucial sector for many developing countries, and the MSD approach can be applied to enhance agricultural value chains. By identifying constraints and opportunities within the agricultural market system, MSD practitioners can work with small-scale farmers, input suppliers, processors, and other market actors to improve productivity, access to inputs and markets, and value addition. This approach can lead to increased incomes, food security, and improved livelihoods for rural communities.

Financial Inclusion and Access to Finance: Access to finance is a significant challenge for many individuals and small businesses in developing economies. The MSD approach can be utilized to address this challenge by promoting financial inclusion and improving access to finance. By working with financial institutions, regulators, and other stakeholders, MSD practitioners can help create an enabling environment that supports the development of inclusive financial systems, facilitates access to credit and savings products, and promotes financial literacy and entrepreneurship.

Employment and Skills Development: Unemployment and underemployment are persistent challenges in many developing countries. The MSD approach can be applied to address these challenges by promoting employment and skills development. By understanding the demand and supply dynamics of the labor market, MSD practitioners can work with employers, training institutions, and government agencies to identify skill gaps, develop relevant training programs, and facilitate job placement. This approach can lead to improved employability, income generation, and poverty reduction.

Trade and Market Access: Access to local, regional, and international markets is crucial for the growth of businesses and economies. The MSD approach can be utilized to address market access barriers and promote fair and inclusive trade. By working with market actors, policymakers, and trade facilitation agencies, MSD practitioners can help identify and address bottlenecks in market systems, enhance trade infrastructure, and promote compliance with quality and safety standards. This approach can lead to increased market opportunities, export diversification, and economic integration.

Micro, Small, and Medium Enterprises (MSMEs) Development: MSMEs play a vital role in job creation, income generation, and poverty reduction. The MSD approach can be applied to support the development of MSMEs by addressing constraints and enhancing their competitiveness. By working with MSMEs, business development service providers, and financial institutions, MSD practitioners can help improve access to technology, finance, and markets, strengthen business linkages, and promote entrepreneurship. This approach can lead to increased productivity, innovation, and sustainable growth of MSMEs.

Women's Economic Empowerment: Gender inequality is a significant barrier to inclusive economic growth. The MSD approach can be utilized to promote women's economic empowerment by addressing gender-specific constraints and promoting gender equality within market systems. By working with women entrepreneurs, policymakers, and civil society organizations, MSD practitioners can help remove barriers to women's participation in markets, improve access to resources and opportunities, and promote gender-responsive policies. This approach can lead to increased women's income, decision-making power, and overall well-being.

The Market System Development approach has diverse applications across various sectors and development challenges. By applying this approach, practitioners can address market failures, promote inclusive growth, and create sustainable economic opportunities for all. Whether it is in agriculture, finance, employment, trade, MSMEs, or women's economic empowerment, the MSD approach offers a comprehensive and flexible framework to drive positive change and achieve long-term development outcomes.

Application of MSD for IDPs

The Market System Development (MSD) approach is a powerful framework that can be applied to address the unique challenges faced by Internally Displaced Persons (IDPs). IDPs are individuals who have been forced to flee their homes due to conflict, violence, or natural disasters, but remain within the borders of their own country. The MSD approach focuses on enhancing market systems to create sustainable economic opportunities for all, including IDPs. In this article, we will explore the application areas of the Market System Development approach specifically for IDPs.

Livelihoods and Income Generation: One of the key challenges faced by IDPs is the loss of livelihoods and income. The MSD approach can be applied to support IDPs in rebuilding their livelihoods and generating sustainable income. By working with local markets, businesses, and relevant stakeholders, MSD practitioners can identify opportunities for IDPs to engage in income-generating activities. This can include skills training, support for entrepreneurship, and facilitating access to markets and finance. By promoting self-reliance and economic empowerment, the MSD approach can help IDPs regain their independence and improve their living conditions.

Access to Basic Services: IDPs often face limited or disrupted access to basic services such as healthcare, education, and clean water. The MSD approach can be utilized to improve access to these services. By working with service providers, government agencies, and humanitarian organizations, MSD practitioners can identify market failures and develop strategies to address them. This can include improving the availability and affordability of essential goods and services, enhancing infrastructure, and strengthening service delivery systems. Through these interventions, the MSD approach can contribute to the well-being and resilience of IDPs.

Shelter and Housing: Safe and adequate shelter is a critical need for IDPs. The MSD approach can be applied to address the challenges related to shelter and housing. By working with construction companies, suppliers, and government agencies, MSD practitioners can identify market gaps and develop innovative solutions. This can include promoting affordable and sustainable housing options, improving access to construction materials, and supporting local businesses involved in the construction sector. Through these interventions, the MSD approach can help IDPs secure safe and dignified living conditions.

Market Integration and Social Cohesion: IDPs often face social exclusion and marginalization. The MSD approach can be utilized to promote market integration and social cohesion among IDPs and host communities. By facilitating dialogue and collaboration between different market actors, MSD practitioners can foster inclusive market systems that benefit both IDPs and the local population. This can include promoting business linkages, supporting market-driven value chains, and encouraging cooperation and trust-building among diverse stakeholders. By promoting economic integration and social cohesion, the MSD approach can contribute to peaceful coexistence and long-term stability.

Access to Justice and Legal Services: IDPs often face challenges in accessing justice and legal services, which can further exacerbate their vulnerability. The MSD approach can be applied to improve access to justice for IDPs. By working with legal aid organizations, justice sector institutions, and community leaders, MSD practitioners can identify barriers and develop strategies to overcome them. This can include providing legal assistance, promoting awareness of rights and legal processes, and strengthening the capacity of justice institutions to address the specific needs of IDPs. Through these interventions, the MSD approach can help ensure that IDPs have access to justice and are able to exercise their rights.

The Market System Development approach has significant potential to address the challenges faced by Internally Displaced Persons. By promoting sustainable economic opportunities, improving access to basic services, supporting shelter and housing solutions, fostering market integration and social cohesion, and enhancing access to justice, the MSD approach can contribute to the well-being and resilience of IDPs. By working in collaboration with relevant stakeholders, MSD practitioners can create positive and lasting change in the lives of IDPs, helping them rebuild their lives and regain their dignity.

Application of MSD for Refugees

The Market System Development (MSD) approach is a powerful framework that can be applied to address the unique challenges faced by refugees. Refugees are individuals who have been forced to leave their home countries due to conflict, persecution, or natural disasters, and seek safety and protection in other countries. The MSD approach focuses on enhancing market systems to create sustainable economic opportunities for all, including refugees. In this article, we will explore the application areas of the Market System Development approach specifically for refugees.

Livelihoods and Income Generation: One of the key challenges faced by refugees is the loss of livelihoods and income. The MSD approach can be applied to support refugees in rebuilding their livelihoods and generating sustainable income. By working with local markets, businesses, and relevant stakeholders, MSD practitioners can identify opportunities for refugees to engage in income-generating activities. This can include skills training, support for entrepreneurship, and facilitating access to markets and finance. By promoting self-reliance and economic empowerment, the MSD approach can help refugees become self-sufficient and contribute to the local economy.

Access to Basic Services: Refugees often face limited access to basic services such as healthcare, education, and shelter. The MSD approach can be utilized to improve access to these services. By working with service providers, government agencies, and humanitarian organizations, MSD practitioners can identify market failures and develop strategies to address them. This can include improving the availability and affordability of essential goods and services, enhancing infrastructure, and strengthening service delivery systems. Through these interventions, the MSD approach can contribute to the well-being and resilience of refugees.

Housing and Shelter: Safe and adequate housing is a critical need for refugees. The MSD approach can be applied to address the challenges related to housing and shelter. By working with construction companies, suppliers, and government agencies, MSD practitioners can identify market gaps and develop innovative solutions. This can include promoting affordable and sustainable housing options, improving access to construction materials, and supporting local businesses involved in the construction sector. Through these interventions, the MSD approach can help refugees secure safe and dignified living conditions.

Market Integration and Social Cohesion: Refugees often face social exclusion and marginalization. The MSD approach can be utilized to promote market integration and social cohesion among refugees and host communities. By facilitating dialogue and collaboration between different market actors, MSD practitioners can foster inclusive market systems that benefit both refugees and the local population. This can include promoting business linkages, supporting market-driven value chains, and encouraging cooperation and trust-building among diverse stakeholders. By promoting economic integration and social cohesion, the MSD approach can contribute to peaceful coexistence and long-term stability.

Access to Education and Skills Development: Access to education and skills development is crucial for refugees to rebuild their lives and contribute to the local economy. The MSD approach can be applied to improve access to quality education and skills training for refugees. By working with educational institutions, vocational training centers, and relevant stakeholders, MSD practitioners can identify barriers and develop strategies to overcome them. This can include providing scholarships, developing tailored training programs, and promoting recognition of skills and qualifications acquired in the refugee context. Through these interventions, the MSD approach can help refugees acquire the knowledge and skills needed to succeed in the job market.

The Market System Development approach has significant potential to address the challenges faced by refugees. By promoting sustainable economic opportunities, improving access to basic services, supporting housing and shelter solutions, fostering market integration and social cohesion, and enhancing access to education and skills development, the MSD approach can contribute to the well-being and resilience of refugees. By working in collaboration with relevant stakeholders, MSD practitioners can create positive and lasting change in the lives of refugees, helping them rebuild their lives, integrate into society, and contribute to their host communities.

Application of MSD for Returnees and Host Communities

The Market System Development (MSD) approach is a powerful framework that can be applied to address the unique challenges faced by returnees and host communities. Returnees are individuals who have returned to their home countries after being displaced due to conflict, while host communities are the local populations that receive and accommodate these returnees. The MSD approach focuses on enhancing market systems to create sustainable economic opportunities for all. In this article, we will explore the application areas of the Market System Development approach specifically for returnees and host communities.

Livelihoods and Economic Recovery: One of the key challenges faced by returnees and host communities is the need to rebuild livelihoods and stimulate economic recovery. The MSD approach can be applied to support both groups in generating sustainable income and creating economic opportunities. By working with local markets, businesses, and relevant stakeholders, MSD practitioners can identify areas for economic growth and develop strategies to promote entrepreneurship and job creation. This can include skills training, support for small and medium-sized enterprises, and facilitating access to finance and markets. By strengthening market systems, the MSD approach can contribute to the economic recovery of returnees and host communities.

Infrastructure Development: Returnees and host communities often face challenges related to infrastructure, such as inadequate transportation, water, and energy systems. The MSD approach can be utilized to address these infrastructure gaps. By working with infrastructure providers, government agencies, and relevant stakeholders, MSD practitioners can identify market failures and develop strategies to improve infrastructure development. This can include promoting public-private partnerships, facilitating investment in infrastructure projects, and supporting local businesses involved in infrastructure development. Through these interventions, the MSD approach can help improve living conditions and enhance economic opportunities for both returnees and host communities.

Access to Basic Services: Returnees and host communities may have limited access to basic services such as healthcare, education, and sanitation. The MSD approach can be applied to improve the availability, affordability, and quality of these services. By working with service providers, government agencies, and humanitarian organizations, MSD practitioners can identify market failures and develop strategies to address them. This can include strengthening healthcare systems, promoting inclusive education, and improving access to clean water and sanitation facilities. Through these interventions, the MSD approach can contribute to the well-being and resilience of returnees and host communities.

Market Integration and Social Cohesion: Returnees and host communities often face social and economic challenges related to integration and cohesion. The MSD approach can be utilized to promote market integration and social cohesion among both groups. By facilitating dialogue and collaboration between different market actors, MSD practitioners can foster inclusive market systems that benefit returnees and host communities alike. This can include promoting business linkages, supporting value chains that involve both groups, and encouraging cooperation and trust-building among diverse stakeholders. By promoting economic integration and social cohesion, the MSD approach can contribute to long-term stability and peaceful coexistence.

Entrepreneurship and Skills Development: Promoting entrepreneurship and skills development is crucial for the economic empowerment of returnees and host communities. The MSD approach can be applied to support the development of entrepreneurship and vocational skills among both groups. By working with training centers, vocational schools, and relevant stakeholders, MSD practitioners can identify skills gaps and develop strategies to address them. This can include providing entrepreneurship training, supporting access to finance for small businesses, and facilitating apprenticeship programs. Through these interventions, the MSD approach can help enhance the capacity of returnees and host communities to participate in the local economy.

The Market System Development approach has significant potential to address the challenges faced by returnees and host communities. By promoting sustainable economic opportunities, supporting infrastructure development, improving access to basic services, fostering market integration and social cohesion, and promoting entrepreneurship and skills development, the MSD approach can contribute to the well-being and resilience of both groups. By working collaboratively with relevant stakeholders, MSD practitioners can drive positive change, helping to rebuild livelihoods, stimulate economic growth, and foster inclusive and prosperous communities for returnees and host populations alike.

www.ingramcontent.com/pod-product-compliance
Lightning Source LLC
Chambersburg PA
CBHW071913210526
45479CB00002B/401